DATE

I AM
SPARTACUS!

MAKING A FILM, BREAKING THE BLACKLIST

I AM SPARTACUS!

MAKING A FILM, BREAKING THE BLACKLIST

KIRK DOUGLAS

INTEGRATED MEDIA

NEW YORK

FOREWORD

THERE'S ONE CONSTANT THAT YOU can find to define a person's character.

It's not how you perform when things are easy; it's how you handle yourself when it's tough.

Everyone can be fearless and forthright when the stakes are low . . . but when it's your livelihood or even your life on the line, or your family's or your friends' . . . that's when you understand the kind of mettle you're made of.

Kirk Douglas' mettle is made of pretty stern stuff. Unlike so many characters we see in movies, he didn't necessarily start out championing a cause. His path to glory rests more at the feet of characters like Atticus Finch in *To Kill a Mockingbird*. He hadn't sought out the fight . . . it found him . . . and like Atticus, he did what he knew he had to . . . what was right.

It's hard to imagine now what the weight of McCarthyism meant to so many. It's difficult to picture loyal Americans pulled before Senate subcommittees and being asked to name their friends' names or go to jail. Being tried in public without the ability to face the charges brought against you . . . a lot of very good people buckled under that weight.

The ones who didn't suffered, long after McCarthy was holding hearings . . . for that matter long after he was even alive.

Dalton Trumbo was one of the most respected writers in Hollywood . . . and continued to write under pen names for years after going to jail for refusing to incriminate his coworkers.

In December 2011, his name was placed where it always should have been . . . as a credited writer on the film *Roman Holiday*.

But long before December 2011, Kirk Douglas stepped out of the dark and, as the producer and star of Stanley Kubrick's *Spartacus*, gave Dalton Trumbo screen credit for the first time since he was brought before the House Un-American Activities Committee.

I guess it sounds small now. A screenwriter getting credit for a film he actually wrote . . . but in the history books, it's marked as the moment that the Hollywood blacklist ended.

Kirk Douglas is many things. A movie star. An actor. A producer. But he is, first and foremost, a man of extraordinary character. The kind that's formed when the stakes are high. The kind we always look for at our darkest hour.

GEORGE CLOONEY

INTRODUCTION

What you learn about yourself with the passing of time can't be taught. It can only be experienced. You can never "know then what you know now."

When I look back at Spartacus *today—more than fifty years after the fact—I'm amazed that it ever happened at all. Everything was against us— the McCarthy-era politics, competition with another picture, everything.*

I am 95 years old. When I was born, Woodrow Wilson was in the White House. I've lived through sixteen presidents, two World Wars, the Great Depression, and a score of political crises from Teapot Dome to Watergate to Bill Clinton's impeachment for being publicly serviced in the White House.

As I write these words, America is more deeply divided than at any point in my lifetime. From its inception, our country has experienced many divisive periods. Of course, the most serious division occurred with the Civil War. More than half a million people were killed and it almost brought about the dissolution of the United States. Yet somehow we've always survived.

What I want to tell you about in this book is what it was like to make the film Spartacus *during another divisive period in our nation's history. The '50s were a time of fear and paranoia. The Communists were the enemy then. Terrorists are the enemy now. The names change, yet the fear remains. That fear is still inflamed by politicians and exploited by the media. They profit by keeping us afraid.*

The first president I ever voted for was Franklin Roosevelt. He said, "We have nothing to fear but fear itself."

I am not a political activist. When I produced Spartacus *in 1959, I was trying to make the best movie I could make, not a political statement. I brought together a cast of some of the finest actors ever to appear on-screen: Laurence Olivier, Charles Laughton, Peter Ustinov, Jean Simmons, and Tony Curtis. I hired a talented young director I knew. At the time, he was still largely unknown to the general public. His name was Stanley Kubrick.*

Let others judge the movie. I believe it stands on its own merits. I am proud of it.

When I talk to my grandchildren about the making of Spartacus, *it seems to them like a fantastic tale from a faraway time—the 1950s. They're right. It was a long time ago. Yet in a world where one man in Tunisia can set off events that topple the government of Egypt, the story of* Spartacus *is as important today as it was fifty years ago— and two thousand years ago.*

A revolutionary spirit is circling the globe. Is it contagious? We are surprised when we see leaderless crowds of people gathering in American cities, speaking with one voice, challenging the power structure that seems impregnable. That was what Spartacus did. And tens of thousands lent their voices to his. Together, they were all Spartacus.

I was a young man when I made this film. I've often said that if I had been a little bit older, I might never have taken it on at all. I certainly don't think that I would have hired Dalton Trumbo to write it under his own name. He was a lightning rod for the country's divisiveness. After almost a year in jail for his political views, he was still on the studios' blacklist—the "Do Not Hire" rule that had been in place for more than a decade.

Some people these days still try to justify the blacklist. They say it was necessary to protect America. They say that the only people who were hurt by it were our enemies.

They are lying. Innocent men, women, and children saw their lives ruined by this national disgrace.

I know. I was there. I watched it happen.

Now I will tell you about it. And about Spartacus*—the movie we made in the midst of all that madness.*

KIRK DOUGLAS
JANUARY 1, 2012

Dalton Trumbo was the highest paid screenwriter in Hollywood when he was called before the House Committee on Un-American Activities in 1947.

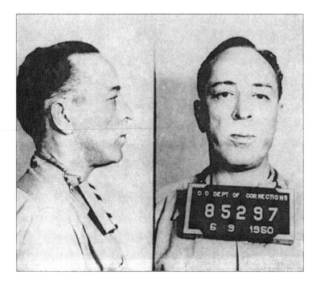

Three years later, he was on his way to federal prison for contempt of Congress.

CHAPTER ONE

"In every city and province, lists of the
disloyal have been compiled."

—Laurence Olivier as Marcus Crassus

IN THE CAUCUS ROOM OF the old House Office Building, the House Committee on Un-American Activities (HUAC) was gaveled to order by Congressman J. Parnell Thomas, Republican of New Jersey. It was Tuesday, October 28, 1947. Ten men, motion picture writers and directors, had been called before the Committee to testify about their current and prior political affiliations.

Nine of them were screenwriters: Dalton Trumbo, Albert Maltz, Ring Lardner Jr., Lester Cole, Alvah Bessie, Herbert Biberman, John Howard Lawson, Samuel Ornitz, and Adrian Scott. One was a director—Edward Dmytryk.

These men—the so-called "Unfriendly Ten"—viewed the

HUAC investigation *itself* as an un-American violation of their First Amendment rights of free speech and free association, and they intended to say so publicly.

The first witness on that cold October day was Dalton Trumbo. He raised his right hand and was asked if he would swear "to give the truth, the whole truth, and nothing but the truth, so help you God."

Trumbo replied, "I do." Yet it quickly became apparent to fair-minded Americans that the only "truth" desired by the Committee (which included an unknown freshman congressman named Richard M. Nixon) was anything—whether true or not—that confirmed their predetermined verdict of these ten men: *guilty.*

Seated directly behind Trumbo in the crowded chamber were members of the Committee for the First Amendment, a Hollywood group created to provide support for the subpoenaed witnesses.

The delegation of film stars that flew to Washington, D.C., on a private plane provided by Howard Hughes, included Humphrey Bogart and his young wife, Lauren Bacall, as well as Gene Kelly, Danny Kaye, John Garfield, and John Huston.

I knew Lauren Bacall from New York. I first met her on a cold winter day in 1940 when we were both struggling students at the American Academy of Dramatic Arts. She was only sixteen years old, just entering the Academy. I was a senior, an "older man" of twenty-three. She was Betty Joan Perske back then. She's still Betty to me now.

Bacall, with a take-no-prisoners honesty that defines her to this day, bluntly described in her autobiography what she saw playing out in front of her in that room:

> When witnesses such as . . . Dalton Trumbo . . . were asked "Are you a member of the Communist Party?" and refused to answer, they were exercising their rights as defined in the Bill of Rights. They wouldn't answer whether they were members

of the Screen Writers' Guild either. Political affiliation was not
the business of the Committee . . . and Thomas was gavel
happy. I couldn't believe what was going on—that jerk sitting
up there with his title had the power to put these men in jail!

J. Parnell Thomas threw down the gauntlet to every witness
who came before his committee, thundering:

The Chairman: Are you or have you ever been a member
of the Communist Party?!
Mr. Trumbo: I believe I have the right to be confronted
with any evidence which supports this question.

What the arrogant Chairman hadn't expected was a witness as
verbally agile and combative as Dalton Trumbo:

The Chairman: Oh. Well you would?
Mr. Trumbo: Yes.
The Chairman: Well you will, pretty soon. [Pounding gavel]
The witness is excused. Impossible!
Mr. Trumbo: This is the beginning . . .
The Chairman: [Pounding gavel] Just a minute!
Mr. Trumbo: . . . of an American concentration camp for
writers!
The Chairman: This is typical Communist tactics! This is
typical Communist tactics! [Pounding gavel]

That officious bastard Thomas whacked his gavel and Dalton
Trumbo was dragged away.

But those hearings were no joke. Dalton Trumbo and the
other Unfriendly Ten literally lost their freedom. They would all
be sent to jail for contempt of Congress.

At this point in my life, I was still an up-and-coming young
actor. Along with millions of Americans, I listened to highlights

of the hearings on the radio. Still a new medium, television didn't cover them. Just a month earlier, I had actually bought my first small set to watch the World Series, the first time it was ever broadcast on TV. Jackie Robinson's Brooklyn Dodgers were playing the New York Yankees. Even on my tiny screen, I couldn't help but be impressed by the grace and talent of this game-changing Negro rookie.

Two years later, Jackie Robinson was also called before the House Committee on Un-American Activities to testify about his association with controversial singer Paul Robeson. Of course, he had none. The only connection they had was that they were both *black*, which was enough for J. Parnell Thomas. It was the era of guilt by association.

I wasn't subpoenaed as a witness, or asked to join with Bacall, Bogart, and the others, because I wasn't a big enough "name" to matter to the newspapers.

At the time, I'd still only made one picture—*The Strange Love of Martha Ivers.*

My memory of that time has a different title: *The Strange Life of Kirk Douglas*. Fresh off the train from New York, I arrived in Hollywood in 1945 with very little awareness of the political controversies that were just starting to affect the movie business. I knew nothing about the first round of HUAC hearings held during the war, while I was overseas in the navy. Nor was I aware that both Robert Rossen, the screenwriter of *The Strange Love of Martha Ivers*, as well as Lewis Milestone, its director, held strong political views that would later get them both in trouble.

Hell, at this point, all I knew was that I was coming out to Hollywood to star in a movie. This is how little anyone told me before I left New York: *I* thought I'd been cast as the romantic lead in the picture, opposite Barbara Stanwyck.

When I got off the train in Los Angeles, I was promptly informed by the studio rep that Mr. Van Heflin would be playing that part, not me. I had been cast in the third lead. All across the country, I'd been studying for the wrong part.

On my first day of shooting, Paramount sent a limousine to pick me up and bring me to the set. I was flabbergasted. That was a big thrill for me. But when the driver pulled up to those big gates on Melrose Avenue, I was stunned to see angry picketers outside.

It was only at that moment that I learned there was a labor strike going on at the studio. This was the latest (and it would turn out to be the last) in a series of strikes involving the major studios and the left-wing Conference of Studio Unions. The unions asked the Screen Actors Guild (SAG) to support the strike. But SAG, led by its president, George Murphy, and executive committee members Ronald Reagan and George Montgomery, refused to cooperate. They encouraged actors to cross the picket lines.

No one had bothered to tell me about any of this before I got out there. It wasn't until later that I learned what the strike was even about—protecting benefits for the set dressers.

One of those picketing outside Paramount was Robert Rossen. The driver pointed him out to me—"That's Bob Rossen, the writer."

I looked down at the script sitting next to me on the seat— Rossen's name was on the cover. The first time I ever laid eyes on him, he was carrying a protest sign.

Inside the studio, I got the next shock. My director, Lewis "Milly" Milestone, wasn't even on the set. As a show of support for the strikers, he was spending the day in Oblath's restaurant across the street. A substitute "director" would handle that day's shooting.

The first motion picture of my career and the director was literally out to lunch. Welcome to Hollywood, Kirk.

Things were so intense that the producer, Hal Wallis, decided I should sleep at the studio, rather than risk being locked out. I slept in my dressing room for the next several nights, until the strike was resolved.

All politics aside, my life would have been much healthier if that director, Lewis Milestone, had never come back. He was a nice guy, but he believed that actors should always do exactly what they were told.

"So, Kirk, in this scene, I think that you should be smoking a cigarette."

"But, Mr. Milestone, I don't smoke."

"That's okay, kid, you'll learn."

I shut up and did what I was told. Right after we finished the scene, I raced to my dressing room and threw up. Unfortunately, that was the only time I got sick from smoking. Milestone was right, I *did* learn. Two packs a day for forty years. Thanks, Milly.

The film turned out all right, although Miss Stanwyck ignored me for the first two weeks of shooting. I got good notices as the third lead, and she eventually told me I'd done a good job. I told *her* that her compliment came "too late." I was a cocky kid.

Two years later, both Milestone and Rossen were subpoenaed by the House Un-American Activities Committee, at the same time that the Unfriendly Ten appeared. Lewis Milestone fled to Paris. Robert Rossen admitted his membership in the Communist Party.

Both were blacklisted.

I didn't know it then, but my first movie was written by a card-carrying Communist. Looking back on it now, I couldn't care less.

I've always wondered what would have happened if I had arrived in Hollywood even five years earlier. Would I have been caught up in the middle of those fights? And if I had, would I have even had a career?

Of course, many people in Hollywood cooperated fully with the HUAC investigations. Ronald Reagan was a friendly witness. So were other actors like Gary Cooper, Robert Montgomery, George Murphy, and Adolphe Menjou.

Menjou told the Committee, "I am a witch hunter if the

witches are Communists. I am a Red baiter. I would like to see them all back in Russia."

Funny thing about Adolphe Menjou: a decade later, when I hired him for a part in *Paths of Glory*, he was more than happy to take a paycheck from Bryna, my production company. I guess nobody told him that it was named after my Russian mother.

The country was deeply frightened and divided, much as it is today. Anti-Semitism was still a big factor. The name "Kirk Douglas" got me work as an actor. The name I was born with—"Issur Danielovitch"—wouldn't have gotten me through the door. Racial prejudice was still the accepted norm. Even though Jackie Robinson had broken the color barrier in baseball, President Truman's decision to integrate the military was still a year away.

But more than anything, it was the growing hysteria about Communism—the "Red Scare"—that shadowed life all across America. To many, it was seen as a real threat. Others believed it as just more fearmongering. But it was never far from our minds.

The same year that I arrived in Hollywood—1945—Gerald L. K. Smith, the religious demagogue and founder of the America First Party, began publicly attacking the "alien-minded Russian Jews in Hollywood."

Cynically, Smith combined anti-Semitism with fear of Communism into one package. Anyone who was Jewish, anyone who was Russian, was a traitor.

Did he mean me? I was a Jew of Russian heritage. My parents emigrated from Belarus. But they never saw themselves as anything but Americans. My mother, who could not read or write in English, taught me to love this country as much as she did. "America," she would say, her voice filled with amazement. "Such a wonderful country!"

I had enlisted in the navy after Pearl Harbor and served in the Pacific with pride. Now here was this vicious anti-Semite, Smith, essentially questioning my loyalty, as well as the patriotism of anyone in Hollywood who was of Jewish or Russian descent.

One month after Dalton Trumbo (who, for the record, was *not* Jewish) appeared before the House Un-American Activities Committee, a group of four dozen top motion picture executives and distributors met privately for two days at the Waldorf-Astoria Hotel.

When their closed-door meetings were over, these great and powerful men issued what came to be known as the "Waldorf Statement." This was the beginning of the Hollywood blacklist. Its key provision declared:

Members of the Association of Motion Picture Producers deplore the action of the 10 Hollywood men who have been cited for contempt by the House of Representatives. We will forthwith discharge or suspend without compensation those in our employ, and we will not re-employ any of the 10 until such time as he is acquitted or has purged himself of contempt and declares under oath that he is not a Communist.

Wow. I need to take a moment here and come up for some air. As I look back on these words more than sixty years later, I feel anger, revulsion, and a deep sadness.

Of the Unfriendly Ten, six were Jewish. I'm sorry to say that most of the men who issued the Waldorf Statement were also Jewish.

How could Jews, who themselves had been the victims of thousands of years of persecution, including the most horrific example of fear and genocide the world has ever known—the Holocaust in Europe—justify perpetuating a similar climate of fear in America?

The answer is found in the question itself. Fear breeds fear. These men—people like Jack Warner, Louis B. Mayer, and Harry Cohn—were terrified their great power would be taken away from them in a heartbeat if their loyalty to America was ever called into question.

So they became superpatriots. And to prove themselves right-minded, they were more than willing to sacrifice the lives of others, even their fellow Jews. They were like the Vichy government in

France, collaborators who held on to their influence and position at the expense of their fellow countrymen.

Hollywood had gone crazy. The witch hunts that Adolphe Menjou had stupidly encouraged were spreading like raging wildfires all across the country. Like most Americans, I watched it happening and felt helpless to stop it.

Fredric March, speaking on the national radio broadcast "Hollywood Fights Back," saw the handwriting on the wall:

> Who do you think they're really after? Who's next? Is it your minister who will be told what he can say in his pulpit? Is it your children's school teacher who will be told what she can say in classrooms? Is it your children themselves? Is it you, who will have to look around nervously before you can say what is on your minds? Who are they after? They're after more than Hollywood. This reaches into every American city and town.

Freddie March got it right. He could see the storm coming. Maybe that's why I chose him to play the president of the United States when I produced *Seven Days in May*.

In the years that followed those hearings, thousands of lives were ruined. Careers were ended with the stroke of a pen, and not just in Hollywood.

Almost three years after the HUAC hearings, in 1950, the Supreme Court refused to hear the appeals of Dalton Trumbo and the other Unfriendly Ten. Their convictions for contempt of Congress were allowed to stand. Dalton began serving ten months in the federal penitentiary in Ashland, Kentucky. His wife and three young children were left without a husband or father to provide for them.

At the same time, in a twist that no screenwriter would have dared to invent, that pompous ass Committee Chairman J. Parnell Thomas was convicted of padding his payroll with phony jobs. He then pocketed the money himself. His defense was essentially that "everybody did it."

That didn't fly with the judge, who sent the now-former Chairman to a federal penitentiary in Danbury, Connecticut. It was also the place where two members of the Unfriendly Ten, Lester Cole and Ring Lardner Jr., were serving their sentences for contempt of Congress. Ironically, they found themselves in prison with the same man who'd put them there.

I often wonder what they said to the once-mighty congressman when they passed him in the prison cafeteria—"Pass the gavel, please"?

Justice may be blind, but sometimes she has a terrific sense of humor.

An obscure Republican senator from Wisconsin, Joseph R. McCarthy, quickly thrust himself into the vacuum left by the imprisonment of J. Parnell Thomas. He began by lying about how he had numerous "lists" of Communists who had infiltrated all walks of American life.

More and more people I knew, including my friend Carl Foreman, the screenwriter, were caught up in a situation that continued to grow uglier and more threatening. We started to call it "McCarthyism"—a new word that the language didn't need.

Like me, Carl was also the son of Russian-Jewish immigrants. He was a brilliant writer. Carl wrote the scripts for two of the pictures that really established me as an actor, *Champion* and *Young Man with a Horn*. (His daughter, Amanda Foreman, is also a tremendous writer. I wish he could have lived to see her success.)

The film for which Carl is most remembered now is *High Noon*. He not only wrote the original screenplay, but coproduced it as well.

In 1951, right in the middle of shooting *High Noon*, Carl was subpoenaed to testify before HUAC. His refusal to name names meant that his career in America was effectively over. He fled to England before he could suffer the same fate as Trumbo and the others. He made it out of the country just before the State Department revoked his passport.

Hedda Hopper, the hate-mongering gossip maven, viciously attacked Carl Foreman, writing in her column that she hoped "he would never be hired here again."

Even the liberal producer Stanley Kramer, one of Carl's closest friends and his business partner, removed Carl's coproducer credit from *High Noon*. He was afraid of what their continued association might cost him in the future.

A few years later, I looked up Carl when I was in London.

We talked for a few minutes, but I sensed something was wrong.

Finally, he said, "It's okay, Kirk."

I had no idea what he was talking about.

"*What's* okay, Carl?"

"It's okay if you don't want to have lunch with me. I understand."

Jesus, I thought. *This is what happens to a guy who thinks all his friends have turned on him.*

"Carl, it's *me*. Kirk. Cut the bullshit. Where do you want to go to lunch?"

I've never forgotten that brief encounter with Carl Foreman. It still reminds me of all the pain caused by the blacklist. Friends turned on friends. Marriages fell apart. Carl's did. He became a man without a country.

In an interview with the American Film Institute years later, Carl wrote these poignant words:

During the so-called McCarthy period . . . my problem was that I felt very alone. I wasn't on anybody's side. I was not a member of the Communist Party at that time, so I didn't want to stand with them, but obviously it was unthinkable for me to be an informer. I knew I was dead; I just wanted to die well.

Some did die.

Philip Loeb was a drama instructor during my student days

in New York. He was a fine teacher; I took several classes from him. Phil's own career, in the new medium of television, was just getting started when they came after him.

In June of 1950, a publication called *Red Channels: The Report of Communist Influence in Radio and Television* listed Philip Loeb as a Communist. He strongly denied it, but his protest of innocence didn't matter to General Foods, the sponsor of his television program. They insisted the network fire him. It did.

He never got work in television again. Solely responsible for the care of his mentally troubled son, he could no longer support him. Phil sank into a deep depression. He overdosed on sleeping pills in 1955.

One reader wrote to the *New York Times* declaring that "Philip Loeb died of a sickness called the blacklist." Although the *Times* printed the letter, shortly after the editors made their own position crystal clear: "We would not knowingly employ a Communist party member in the news or editorial departments . . . because we would not trust his ability to report the news objectively or to comment on it honestly."

Ironically, the same month that Phil Loeb was first black-listed—June 1950—similar events played out in the lives of two other men.

They didn't know each other, and I didn't know either of them. Not yet.

They were Dalton Trumbo and a novelist named Howard Fast.

Howard Fast was one of the most successful historical novelists in America. His books included *The Unvanquished*, *Citizen Tom Paine*, and *Freedom Road*. At this point in his life, Fast was also an unapologetic Communist.

Early in 1950, Fast was called to Washington, D.C., to testify before HUAC (now chaired by a Democrat, John Wood of Georgia). The issue was Fast's past support for an anti-Franco group, the Joint Anti-Fascist Refugee Committee. Wood and HUAC wanted the names of all their donors. Fast refused to give them up. (One of those he protected was Eleanor Roosevelt.)

Like Dalton Trumbo, Fast was cited for contempt of Congress. He received a three-month sentence and was sent to a federal prison camp in West Virginia. He began serving his term on June 7, 1950.

It was a tough place, but it had a library. And as he later wrote in his memoir *Being Red,* Fast used it:

> . . . there in prison I began to think of Spartacus, the slave . . . I read every scrap and thread of information that I could find in that small prison library. I read whatever there was about Rome—precious little . . . I found the story of Spartacus—and became convinced that there was a way to tell it so that it could at least approximate the truth.

Only two hundred miles away from where Howard Fast was confined, Dalton Trumbo was serving his own contempt sentence in Ashland, Kentucky.

His "name" became Federal Prisoner #7551.

Trumbo never made any apologies for himself or for his actions. After his release he wrote this to a friend:

> . . . show me the man who informs on friends who have harmed no one, and who thereafter earns money he could not have earned before, and I will show you not a decent citizen, not a patriot, but a miserable scoundrel who will, if new pressures arise and the price is right, betray not just his friends but his country itself.

What happened to Dalton Trumbo and Howard Fast that summer set in motion a sequence of events that would profoundly change my life.

But I didn't know it then.

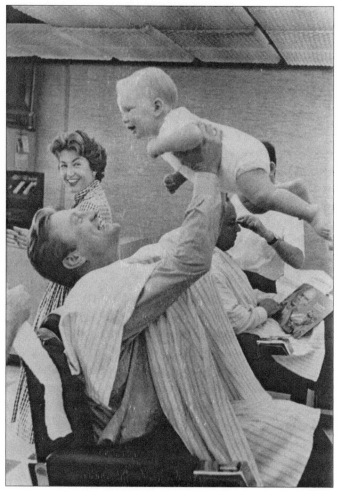

My family was very lucky. I was never blacklisted.

CHAPTER TWO

"Good luck, and may fortune smile upon . . . most of you."

—Peter Ustinov as Lentulus Batiatus

IN THE SUMMER OF 1950, both Dalton Trumbo and Howard Fast were languishing in dank prison cells, thousands of miles from their homes and families. Each man had to be wondering what the future had in store for him.

The fear that caused their imprisonment was still on the rise. Another round of congressional hearings aimed at Hollywood was already being planned. But, looking back on it with some distance—and I'm almost ashamed to admit it—my own life couldn't have been much better. I was untouched by the black-list and, frankly, I wasn't thinking a lot about it. The world was in turmoil—a hot war in Korea, a cold war with the Soviets, suspicion and division in America—yet I was lucky. None of that was affecting me.

The big events happening in my life were all on the home front. I was thirty-three years old and married to a beautiful girl named Diana Dill, another of my classmates from the American Academy of Dramatic Arts. She was so beautiful that she had appeared on the cover of *Life*. Somehow I got a hold of a copy of the magazine while I was in the navy. I showed it to my shipmates and told them I was going to marry her.

I did and we had two wonderful boys, Michael and Joel. (Our marriage didn't survive, but our family did. Diana and I remain good friends. My wife, Anne, calls her "*our* ex-wife.")

By 1950, believe it or not, I was a bona fide movie star. I had played everything from a boxer to a police detective to a trumpet player. *Champion*, my eighth film, had been released in 1949. It earned me my first Academy Award nomination for Best Actor. Even the tough *New York Times* critic Bosley Crowther had positive things to say about me: "Kirk Douglas does a good, aggressive job . . ."

And the money! My God. I was making more money than I'd ever dreamed of. My six sisters and I grew up during the Depression era. Our family struggled every day for bread and borscht. My mother struggled every day with my father.

Home was Amsterdam, New York, a small city north of Albany. When I was growing up, it was known primarily for carpet making. If you didn't have a job at one of the two big carpet companies— Bigelow-Sanford or Mohawk Mills—you had a hard time getting by. My father worked as a ragman, riding up and down the streets of Amsterdam collecting rags and scrap metal for resale. What money he did make often went to the saloons instead of to our family.

Now I was earning more in one year—in one *picture*—than my father made in his entire life.

In Kentucky, Dalton Trumbo was earning only prison wages.

Just a few years earlier, he had been Hollywood's highest-paid screenwriter at $75,000 a picture. Although he was no longer pitching projects to Howard Hawks or Victor Fleming, his eloquent voice was still being heard, at least by those who cared to listen. During his many months alone in that tiny cell, he wrote poignantly about his confinement. He was as candid as ever. This letter was sent to his wife, Cleo:

> Two days hence will be our thirteenth wedding anniversary and I have been lying here on my bunk, thinking about it . . . more and more I realize that when I emerge from here, I must make the choice of what kind of writer I want to be. I think it would be better for all of us if I returned to writing novels, with the occasional foray into theater. It will probably take years to recover from the blow dealt by the blacklist.

Sadly, he was proven right.

Howard Fast was released from prison on August 29, 1950. Never a heavy man, he was now twenty-eight pounds lighter. Like Dalton Trumbo, Fast had been thinking a lot about his writing career. But unlike Trumbo, never for an instant did he consider changing it.

He had always been a novelist. He was determined to remain one.

Fast spent the next nine months writing what he hoped would become his magnum opus—a novel he called *Spartacus*. Plunging himself into the research, he made an extensive study of slavery and the methods of imprisonment practiced in ancient Rome.

He did this even as his own freedom as an American citizen was being systematically reduced and restricted. All in the name of keeping America "safe."

Even when Fast finished serving his sentence and was technically a "free man," his political views still cost him. He was banned from speaking on college campuses. He was under constant surveillance. J. Edgar Hoover took a personal interest in his activities—Fast's FBI file grew to over eleven hundred pages.

When he wanted to travel to Italy to do primary research on the life of Spartacus, Fast was denied a passport. It would be ten years until he was able to obtain one.

Despite all these obstacles, Howard Fast finished *Spartacus* in June of 1951.

Writing the book was the easy part. Selling it was not. The blacklist had found its way into the publishing business as well.

Fast sent *Spartacus* to Little, Brown, the respected New England literary house that had published three of his previous books. After reading the manuscript, the editor was excited and eager to take it on, but a few weeks later, he called Fast back to say the house was passing. Fast soon found out why. As it happened, an FBI agent had been sent to Boston to meet with the president of Little, Brown. Privately, he had "advised" him not to publish *anything* written by Howard Fast. If he did, the agent went on to say, action would be taken against his company. These instructions, the Little, Brown executive was told, came directly from J. Edgar Hoover.

Six more publishing houses turned *Spartacus* down. Fast was left with no alternative but to publish it himself. He and his wife turned their New York City basement into a shipping room and within four months they had printed and sold forty-eight thousand hardcover copies of *Spartacus*. Out of his basement!

The "unbiased" critics ridiculed the book as poorly written, even though Fast's other books were highly praised and had sold millions of copies around the world. The *New York Times* writer couldn't figure out why Fast even bothered to write it, since "every schoolboy knows by now that Roman civilization began to suffer from dry rot long before the advent of the Caesars."

Replying to that critic in *Being Red* many years after the fact, Fast wrote:

It would be a safe bet to say that before the appearance of my book and the film that Kirk Douglas made from it ten years later, not one schoolboy in ten thousand had ever heard of Spartacus.

While Howard Fast was shipping copies of *Spartacus* out of his basement, Dalton Trumbo was finally released from the federal penitentiary in Kentucky. Almost immediately he took Cleo and their three children and moved to Mexico.

I heard about this in the same way we all did, in hushed tones and whispered conversations.

"Did you hear about Dalton Trumbo?"

"Yeah, Mexico, I think."

"That poor bastard."

"Those poor kids."

"I hear Eddie Dmytryk is cooperating now."

"Well, what would *you* do if you were him?"

That was a question I didn't have to answer, except for myself. No one was questioning my patriotism or keeping me from finding work. What *would* I have done if that had suddenly changed? Although Diana and I were, by this point, divorced, I was still responsible for two young children. Would I give up my career on principle? Go to jail?

Eddie Dmytryk did. At least it started out that way.

Like Dalton Trumbo, Dmytryk, an Oscar-nominated director whose nickname was "Mr. RKO," was one of the original Unfriendly Ten. He had also refused to cooperate with HUAC. And he, too, was jailed for contempt of Congress in the same West Virginia penitentiary as Howard Fast.

On September 9, 1950, five days after his forty-second birthday, and after having spent months in prison, Dmytryk finally had enough. The warden witnessed his statement:

> . . . in view of the troubled state of current world affairs I find myself in the presence of an even greater duty and that is . . . to make it perfectly clear that I am not now nor was at

the time of the hearings . . . a member of the Communist
Party . . . and that I recognize the United States of America
as the only country to which I owe allegiance and loyalty.

Despite renouncing his views, he wasn't released until
December. Eddie Dmytryk returned to California a chastened
man. He *had* been a Communist once, but he had no use
for them anymore. Eddie's attorney was Bartley Crum, a liberal Republican who later committed suicide because he, too,
became tainted as a Commie sympathizer. Even Republicans
weren't safe from this guilt-by-association madness.

Crum believed that the best way to get Dmytryk off the blacklist was by returning him to the scene of his "crime." So on April
25, 1951, Eddie Dmytryk once again testified before the House Un-
American Activities Committee. This time he identified twenty-
six people as having been members of the Communist Party.

One of those he named was a writer named Arnold Manoff,
whose wife, a twenty-three-year-old actress named Lee Grant, had
made her film debut a month earlier in a picture called *Detective
Story.* I was the lead. She had a small part; she played a shoplifter.

Lee was only a kid, a beautiful young girl with extraordinary talent and a big future. You could see it. She was so good that she earned
a Best Supporting Actress nomination for her very first film role.

But because Eddie Dmytryk named her husband, Lee Grant
was blacklisted before her film career even had a chance to
begin. Of course, she refused to testify about the man to whom
she was married, and it took years before anyone would hire her
for another picture.

One day, Charlie Feldman—the top man at Famous Artists
Agency—called and asked me for a favor. This was a first for me.
Before I hit it big with *Champion*, Charlie often kept me waiting
for hours when we had an appointment. I'd be told he was too
busy—come back another time.

So when your agent calls and asks *you* for a favor, it's one of those moments when you look at the phone in your hand like you've never seen it before. You think to yourself, *How did it come to* this?

"Kirk, I need you to do me a favor."

"Name it, Charlie."

"You know that director Eddie Dmytryk? He's a client of ours and I'm trying to put a deal together for him with Harry Cohn at Columbia. It's not going to be easy . . . I'm pulling a lot of strings. I think we can get it for him, but it's gonna take some time."

I was silent. I had played a fighter. I could see a punch coming.

Feldman threw it. "Can you help him find something, Kirk? He needs work *now*. He's got a new wife and a young family. His ex-wife took him for everything in the divorce and this whole Commie thing . . ."

"Done. Have him call me."

"You mean it?!"

"Of course I mean it. I've got a lot of scripts that need reading. I can use the help."

Charlie exhaled. "Thanks, Kirk. But you know . . . "

"Know what?"

"There are a lot of people still pissed off at him. I wouldn't want you to get caught up in any of that."

"Charlie, I'm a big boy. You've already sold me the car—now stop kicking the tires. Have him call me."

Eddie Dmytryk came to work for me. He helped me with scripts. I took him out to dinner, to football games, to social gatherings. I wasn't afraid to be seen with him in public.

Eventually, he got a movie and then Stanley Kramer signed him to a multipicture deal. (Yes, the same Stanley Kramer who bailed out on Carl Foreman. Maybe he was feeling guilty.)

After that I never heard from Eddie. Not even a postcard.

Fast-forward to 1953. I'm in Israel making *The Juggler* for . . . Stanley Kramer. He can't wait for me to meet our director. Yeah, you guessed it. His name was Eddie.

The funny part is that Dmytryk never told Stanley that we'd met before. The job, the dinners, the games—all that had apparently slipped his mind in only a few years. So who was *I* to bring it up?

That was sixty years ago. If I knew then that he had named names, I'm not sure I would have given Eddie Dmytryk anything more than a swift kick in the ass. It's one thing to protect your family, or even yourself. That I can understand. But ruining other people's lives just to get your old job back?

Orson Welles put it best: "Friend informed on friend not to save their lives, but to save their swimming pools."

While I was in Tel Aviv shooting *The Juggler* for the now-employable Eddie Dmytryk, Dalton Trumbo was still living in Mexico City. He was part of a colony of other blacklisted writers that included Ring Lardner Jr. and Albert Maltz.

Trumbo was reduced to writing stories for women's magazines under his wife's maiden name. One editor wrote back, impressed, saying that "she" had real talent and should consider writing as a career. Years later, Dalton could finally joke with me about that story.

You need to understand one essential truth about Dalton Trumbo: he *needed* to write. It was as integral to his nature as breathing, maybe more. This is a man who exercised by walking around his pool while chain-smoking.

Even while on the blacklist, Dalton continued to smoke, drink, and churn out stories and screenplays at an astonishing rate. None of them, however, could safely bear the name "Trumbo." So he invented as many as a dozen other names for his work, which was then "fronted" for him by sympathetic friends.

One of those friends, the writer Ian McLellan Hunter, shopped around an original story of Trumbo's, a romantic comedy about a princess who falls in love with a reporter. I still didn't know Trumbo at this point, but I'd just finished shooting *Detective Story* with William Wyler who told me that this script—the title was *Roman Holiday*—had come to him after Frank Capra passed on directing it.

"Why did Capra pass?" I asked Willy. "It sounds like a great story and you'd get to shoot it in Rome."

I had never been to Europe, but my close friend and business adviser, Sam Norton, was encouraging me to make movies out of the country. There were apparently tax breaks you could get by living abroad for long stretches.

Wyler had heard this too, but business wasn't what was on his mind. It was politics.

"Capra passed because he smelled a Red," replied Willy. "He thinks this story was written by some guy on the blacklist and he wants no part of it." He ran his hand through his thick black hair and stared off into the middle distance. Finally, he spoke again; his tone had turned pensive.

"It's starting up again, Kirk. You saw what happened with Eddie Dmytryk."

Wyler was one of the most successful, respected directors in the history of the business. He'd been one of the founders of the Committee for the First Amendment. He wasn't afraid of anybody. Yet here he was thinking about whether doing a picture about a princess and a reporter might get him into trouble with the United States Congress.

This was insanity. Before I could say that, Wyler sent a chill up my spine, "I hear that Gadg might cooperate too."

"Gadg" was Elia Kazan. The following year Kazan named eight names, including the playwright Clifford Odets. Wyler was on a plane to Rome almost immediately after that, having concluded that there was more to be gained by leaving the country during this new round of inquisitions.

A few months later, I began my own odyssey abroad. I did *The Juggler* in Israel, *Act of Love* in Paris, and *Ulysses* in Rome. Sam Norton was wrong. There were no tax benefits from working abroad, but I didn't know that then. Nor would I have cared.

I was head over heels in love with a twenty-year-old Italian actress named Pier Angeli. Or so I thought. We got engaged soon after we met.

She was all that I thought about, morning, noon, and night. (Only later did I discover that while Pier might have been thinking about me in the morning, she was also thinking about several other men in the afternoon and evening.)

Who was it who said that life is what happens to you when you're busy making other plans?

I *did* meet the love of my life in Europe. But it wasn't Pier Angeli.

Her name was Anne Buydens. She was born in Germany and grew up in Belgium and Switzerland. We met in Paris while I was shooting *Act of Love*, and we were married in the United States on May 29, 1954. I have never loved anyone more than I do Anne. In fact, she *is* my life. She's saved it in more ways than I can count and continues to do so every day.

When Anne and I returned to the United States, the political climate was starting to shift back from the near hysteria that had gripped the country when I'd left. Senator Joe McCarthy's wild accusations of Communist infiltration had begun to backfire. He took on the United States Army in nationally televised hearings, which finally revealed him for the vicious demagogue that he was.

Even newlyweds like Anne and me watched on TV. We sat mesmerized when, on June 9, 1954, the army's chief counsel, Joseph Welch, looked straight at McCarthy and asked him: "Have you no sense of decency, sir? At long last, have you left no sense of decency?"

Finally, the American people realized that he did not. For the first time that summer, a majority told the Gallup poll they disapproved of the senator from Wisconsin. His colleagues, now free of the fear that one of them could be his next target, voted overwhelmingly to condemn him in December. He remained in the Senate, a broken man.

President Eisenhower coined the term "McCarthy-*wasm*" to

describe the long-awaited end of this evil man's crusade of terror and intimidation. But the blacklist survived—Hollywood hell-bent on persecuting itself.

January 1, 1955. The New Year dawned with great promise. After spending most of the last two years traveling the world, I was finally back in the United States. I woke up that morning with my beautiful new wife at my side. We had bought a home on San Ysidro Drive in Beverly Hills—a small place, more like a bachelor pad, with barely enough room for Michael and Joel when they came from New York. Anne and I would quickly start looking for a bigger place, with an eye to expanding our family in the near future.

We didn't have long to wait. Anne soon told me that we'd be expecting our first child in November.

My family was starting to grow. The country was coming to its senses.

I decided to take a chance on something that I'd been wanting to do for a long time. I would finally become my own boss.

The studio system was weakening. Independent producers like Stanley Kramer and the Mirisch brothers were developing pictures and then getting studios like United Artists to finance them. Now some actors were doing the same thing, cutting out the middlemen and developing their own projects. Before I had much time to consider the risks, I was one of them.

My friend Burt Lancaster paved the way, with his partner Harold Hecht. By a stroke of luck, Hecht-Lancaster hired a television writer named Paddy Chayevsky to write a small picture about a lonely, unattractive butcher named Marty. It won an Oscar for Ernie Borgnine and was named the Best Picture of 1955. Before he knew it, Burt was no longer just a movie star— he was making *other* people into stars.

I made my decision. I started my own production company. The name was easy. I called it "Bryna," my mother's original Russian name.

When she heard what the company would be called, Ma, who could barely read or write a word of English, wrote me this note (almost certainly with the help of one of my sisters):

God bless you my son. Mother.

I will leave that note to my grandchildren. It will help them understand the miracles that this simple woman witnessed in her lifetime.

I interviewed a lot of people to come work for me at my new company. The first one I hired was a young producer named Eddie Lewis. He made me an offer that I couldn't refuse: "Kirk, I want this job. I'll work for you for free."

The first Bryna production was a western called *Indian Fighter*. I would star in it, along with a new film actor named Walter Matthau. Matthau was a trained stage actor, very successful on Broadway.

We got on well. Like me, Walter was the son of Russian immigrants. There we were, two Jewish cowboys from New York riding horses together on a wilderness trail in Oregon.

This is how good an actor Walter was. His first two pictures were westerns and he *hated* horses. He was afraid of them. Every time Walter got up on a horse, he'd start cursing . . . in Yiddish: "Goddamn, mamzer! You worthless piece of drek, you should be in a glue factory!"

But on film, he was as convincing as Tom Mix. Brilliant actor, funny guy.

We were shooting the picture on location in Oregon. I'd already cast my ex-wife, Diana, for an important supporting role. But we still needed an exotic beauty for the part of the Indian maiden, my character's romantic interest.

While my staff was scrambling to find just the right girl, Anne was at home looking through *Vogue*. She saw a picture of a model, a beautiful young Italian girl named Elsa Martinelli.

Anne showed me the magazine. "Don't you think she would make a fantastic Indian girl?"

I tracked down Elsa in New York City. She could barely speak English and, more to the point, she didn't believe it was *me* on the phone.

In order to convince her that I *was* me, she insisted that I sing her the song from *20,000 Leagues Under the Sea*. She had seen the picture that afternoon.

I cleared my throat and looked at Anne. She was grinning ear to ear, as if to say, "*You're* the one who wanted to be a producer." I stuck my tongue out at her and started auditioning, over the long-distance wire, for the part of *myself*:

Got a whale of a tale to tell ya, lads
A whale of a tale or two
'Bout the flapping fish and girls I've loved
On nights like this with the moon above
A whale of a tale and it's all true,
I swear by my tattoo.

Apparently swearing by my tattoo convinced Elsa, because she got on the next plane to California. We gave her a screen test and put her under contract. Elsa Martinelli was now an Indian maiden and Anne had provided the feathers.

What a woman. She was willing to let me go on location with my ex-wife to shoot a picture in the middle of the wilderness, and she also found the beautiful young actress to play my love interest.

Wait a minute, that's not all. Anne even stayed behind in Los Angeles to take care of eight-year-old Joel and ten-year-old Michael, because both their father *and* their mother were off making a movie.

That's why, when you see the end credits of *Indian Fighter*, the name Anne Buydens is listed as "Casting Supervisor."

Her actual screen credit should have read: "Saint."

When I got back from Oregon, Bryna was in full swing. We were developing a list of other properties. Sam Norton strongly encouraged me to make some pictures that I *didn't* star in. He said that there were business benefits to be gained by doing so. Bryna put three films into production that had no parts for me. I was lucky to have a close friend who was always watching out for my best interests.

The movie I *really* wanted to make—and star in—was based on Irving Stone's novel about Vincent van Gogh. It was called *Lust for Life*. I tried to buy it and was hugely disappointed when I learned that MGM already owned the rights. It wouldn't be a Bryna production. I didn't care. I still intended to play that role, whether I produced it or not.

There was one hitch—a big one. MGM told me I could have the part, *but* I'd have to sign a loyalty oath first.

A *what*?! I was furious. John Houseman, the film's producer, tried to calm me down.

"Now, Kirk," he said in the professorial manner that he would later make famous in *The Paper Chase*. "It's just a formality."

"Formality, my ass!" Before I realized it, I was yelling.

"Those bastards are questioning my patriotism! Tell Louis Mayer he can shove it!"

Houseman was totally unaffected by my anger. He didn't try to argue with me. He simply asked, "Kirk, do you want the part or not?"

That stopped me. I was breathing hard, like a runner who had just pushed himself farther than he thought he could go.

I suddenly realized that I might have gone *too* far.

I wanted that part. I wanted it bad. So what was the problem? I had served in the navy. I *was* loyal to my country. It was only a piece of paper.

I signed it. But I still felt like a fink.

There was no time to think about it. I was quickly learning what my own life was going to be like now that I was "the boss." Studios, lawyers, agents, even other actors . . . everybody wanted a piece of me. And they wanted it *right now*.

Even my kids wanted more from me. I compensated by trying to think of fun things for us to do together as a family. Of course, most of them also involved my work.

I'd made *20,000 Leagues Under the Sea* for Walt Disney and had gotten to know him. Everyone, all over the country, got to know him not long after, in 1955, when he opened Disneyland. Walt's passion for everything that moved wasn't confined to the amusement park. He was in love with railroads and had a life-size system at his house. There were tracks and bridges, even a real engineer. "Uncle Walt" (as he liked to be called) invited me to bring my boys over to ride his trains. They had a great time.

What surprised me was that Walt filmed the whole thing and then used it without telling me. A few weeks later, I saw my family on his TV program, then called "Disneyland." It was all a big commercial for his new amusement park, starring me and my kids. Sam Norton insisted that I sue him, so I did. Then Anne said, "Are you crazy? Even if you win, you lose. Everybody loves Walt Disney." I dropped the suit.

Looking back, this incident shows me two important things about myself.

The first is that Anne's instincts about people are better than mine.

The second, perhaps related to the first, is that I can get along with people whose political views are very different from mine. Walt Disney was a deeply conservative man. Some even say he was an anti-Semite. I never saw that, but I know he hated Communists. He enthusiastically cooperated with J. Parnell Thomas' Hollywood witch hunts.

Still, I liked the guy. Even if he did exploit my kids.

I never let politics get in the way of a friendship. John Wayne and I couldn't have been more different politically. He was a die-hard Republican. I've always been a strong Democrat—but I don't hate Republicans. I've never been a Communist, but I don't hate them either. I think that's what America is about.

When John Wayne died, his son called and told me, "My father really loved you." I was very moved.

Our own son, Peter Douglas, was born on November 23, 1955. His father was deeply immersed in playing the part of Van Gogh. Peter's middle name could only be Vincent.

Over the next year, two unrelated events occurred that would have a lasting impact on my life and career. At the time, I had no clue about their significance to me.

The first happened in faraway Russia, land of my forebears.

Joseph Stalin had ruled the Soviet Union with an iron fist for a dozen years. When he died in 1953, his successor, Nikita Khrushchev, began to explore the truth about Stalin's reign of terror. In February of 1956, Khrushchev issued a secret document called "On the Personality Cult and Its Consequences." It detailed Stalin's tyrannical behavior, including his systematic persecution of Russia's Jews.

Howard Fast, recipient of the 1953 Stalin Peace Prize, was horrified by these revelations. To the delight of American right-wingers, he openly broke with the Communist Party. I didn't know it then, but Fast's highly visible rehabilitation as a "good American" now meant that our paths would cross in a meaningful way. But not quite yet.

The second event that changed my life took place much closer to home than Moscow. Sometime in the summer of 1956, Anne and I saw a movie. It was a little black-and-white film, obviously made on a small budget. It starred Sterling Hayden and was the story of a man who robs a racetrack. What was startling about it was the way it was shot. You felt like you were right there, in the middle of the action.

I watched the credits carefully. "Written and Directed by Stanley Kubrick."

I wanted to meet the guy. I called his agent, Ronnie Lubin.

"Ronnie, tell me about Stanley Kubrick."

"What do you want to know?"

"How old is this guy?"

"He's twenty-eight."

"Twenty-eight?"

"Well, almost."

"He's a talented kid. Have him come see me, Ronnie."

I hung up the phone and looked over at Eddie Lewis, who had been listening to my end of the conversation. Eddie had proven to be a big asset to Bryna. Of course, I put him on a salary right from the start. (Our running joke was, "If I don't pay you, how can I fire you?")

"Eddie," I said, "this may be the guy. Let's see what else he's got."

Our first meeting was cordial. Stanley's demeanor was always calm, impassive. We were both Jews from New York, but this was no Walter Matthau. You could never call him warm.

What I remember most about Kubrick was his eyes. He looked like a basset hound, with those big, sad pouches. What I didn't understand at that first meeting was that his sleepy appearance belied a man who was always awake, always thinking.

"So, what have you guys got going?" I asked. His business partner, Jimmy Harris, was also in the meeting.

Stanley responded with a question of his own. "Have you ever read a book called *Paths of Glory*?"

I shook my head.

He handed me a script with that title. The cover was unusual. It was a photograph of a group of young men in the woods, dressed up in what appeared to be World War I military uniforms.

"Are these French soldiers?" I asked.

"They're actors, dressed up to look like French soldiers," replied Stanley. With a sly smile, he added, "I shot that photo."

I took it home and read it that night. It knocked me out.

Stanley was my first call the next morning.

"You wrote this?" I asked.

"Yes," he answered, calm as always. "With Jim Thompson and Calder Willingham."

"Stanley, I love this picture! We are going to make it! It will never make a nickel, but we *have* to make it!"

And that was how Stanley Kubrick came into my life.

Paths of Glory was set to shoot in the spring of 1957. My company and I had already committed to a big-budget epic called *The Vikings*, with Richard Fleischer directing. The plan was now to shoot them back-to-back at the same studio in Germany, thereby saving on cost.

While Howard Fast was recanting and Stanley Kubrick was turning twenty-eight, Dalton Trumbo was about to earn another Oscar. Yet he still couldn't claim it in his own name.

By this time, Trumbo had moved his family back to the United States. They'd found a small house in the Los Angeles suburb of Highland Park, about twenty minutes east of Hollywood. He was still writing constantly, still using real people as "fronts" to sell his work. He invented enough pseudonyms to fill an address book. The different names helped Trumbo remember which of his many projects a producer might be calling him about. These noms de plume included "Marcel Klauber," "Ben L. Perry," and a married couple, "James and Dorothy Bonham."

The "Bonhams" were how Trumbo collected his money. Dozens of people endorsed checks over to "Jim" or "Dorothy" in order to preserve Dalton's anonymity.

Even though the now-disgraced Senator McCarthy drank himself to death by the end of 1957, these ridiculous deceptions were still necessary to protect people's lives and livelihoods. What Brutus said of Caesar was also true of Joe McCarthy: "The evil that men do lives after them . . ."

Inspired by his time in Mexico, Dalton Trumbo wrote a story, "The Boy and the Bull." It became a feature film called *The Brave One*. The screen credit for Original Story was given to "Robert Rich," Dalton's latest alter ego.

This proved particularly embarrassing to Hollywood when "Robert Rich" actually *won* the Academy Award. On the night that *Roman Holiday* took the prize, a real person—Ian McLellan Hunter—could go up and claim the statue (even though he felt terrible doing it). When *The Brave One* was named the winner, there was no Robert Rich in the house.

On the night of the ceremony in 1957, I was thousands of miles away in Germany. We had just started shooting *Paths of Glory*. My performance in *Lust for Life* had earned me a Best Actor nomination. I was told I was the favorite to win.

Not so. The photographers in my hotel lobby scattered quickly when word arrived that Yul Brynner had won for *The King and I*.

I did, however, win something that night when, after all the hoopla was over, I got a knock on my hotel room door. When I answered, a man handed me a package. I opened it. There was an Oscar inside! Had the news somehow been wrong?

Then I read the inscription, "To Daddy, who rates an Oscar with us always. Stolz and Peter."

"Stolz" was Anne. It's what I call her, the German word for "proud." She had worked through the night to make this happen—to make sure I knew how much I was appreciated by the people who truly mattered to me.

I had just received an "Oscar" that I didn't win. But Dalton Trumbo, watching on television, saw an award that he deserved, an award that he had *won,* go unclaimed. All because his name couldn't be spoken out loud in public.

That was finally going to change. I was about to meet a man named "Sam Jackson."

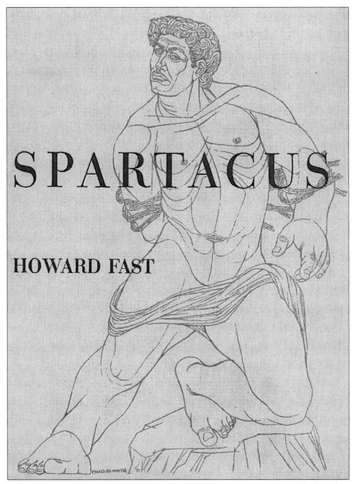

No publishing house would touch Howard Fast's novel
Spartacus *because he was an avowed Communist.*
He published it himself.

CHAPTER THREE

"You don't want to know my name.
I don't want to know your name."

—Woody Strode as Draba

I'VE ALWAYS HATED DESKS.

They symbolize a stern authority figure judging me from on high. Sizing me up. Appraising me. Of course, I'm never good enough—"Sorry, Kirk, you're not right for the part."

Whatever the source of my phobia, it's stayed with me all my life. Today, whenever I go into the Bryna Company, I pull up a chair next to my assistant's desk. She places my correspondence at the corner of her desk, which is my space.

The big office down the hall, the one that *does* have a large desk in it, belongs to Anne, the president of Bryna. I love watching my wife sit behind it with confidence and command.

In the early years of Bryna, I had a big desk. I thought that I needed to prove I was the boss, to show everybody I was in charge. In those days, Anne was still at home taking care of our small child. Peter was just two. And soon we had another one on the way. Anne wouldn't be able to take over the reins of the company for a number of years. By the way, short of marrying her, making Anne president of my company is the smartest decision I've ever made.

My forty-first birthday—Monday, December 9, 1957. I was whistling when I walked into Bryna that morning.

"Happy birthday, Kirk!" came the greetings as I passed through the office. When I got to my desk, a few wrapped gifts were already waiting for me, along with an ornate, handwritten card from my mother.

I sat down in my "big boss" chair. What a lucky guy. *The Vikings* was in postproduction and looking great. Arthur Krim, the president of United Artists, would be releasing it in the spring. They were pushing me hard for another big Bryna project, perhaps even another historical epic.

I picked up the phone and called my mother in upstate New York to thank her for my card. She loved hearing my voice over the phone, but worried about how expensive the call was.

"Hi, Ma!"

"Issur, my birthday boy. Are you warm enough?"

"Ma, it's seventy degrees here. It's not Albany. I'm in California."

No snow in the winter! It must have seemed like a miracle to her. She had never been to California. I could never get her on an airplane.

"You look so thin in your last picture. I'll send you some borscht."

"Ma, don't send me borscht."

"You don't *like* my borscht?"

"Ma, there's no market for fat actors."

As I was saying good-bye to my mother, I heard something land with a loud thud on my desk. I swiveled around in my chair, expecting another gift.

Instead, it was a book.

Eddie Lewis looked back as he walked out of the office. "Happy birthday, Kirk. There's your next project."

I picked it up. *Spartacus*, by Howard Fast. Heavy. I opened it to the end—363 pages.

I knew only some basic facts about the legend of Spartacus who lived before Christ was born and led a slave rebellion against the Roman Empire. I took the book home with me. It kept me up half the night, long after Anne had fallen asleep.

In the morning, I asked Eddie what it would cost to option the book. I was sure it would be expensive—blacklist or not, Howard Fast's novels had sold millions of copies—but I wanted it.

"One hundred dollars," he said, smiling slightly.

"You're kidding me, right?"

"No, I'm not," he said, plainly serious now. "But there's a catch. Fast wants to write the screenplay himself."

That could be a problem. Good authors are notoriously bad screenwriters. Scott Fitzgerald, Theodore Dreiser, Sinclair Lewis—all failed to master the craft. I didn't know Howard Fast. Maybe he would be the exception. I'd heard him described as "brilliant." Only later would I discover that the description originated with him.

The token option was not the risk. It would cost many thousands more to use Fast as the writer. *That* was the real gamble. But United Artists was begging me for another big picture. They'd back my play.

"Eddie, make the deal. We can spare the hundred dollars." I was smug.

As 1958 began, things looked really good for me.

The Vikings would hit theaters in June as a big summer picture.

I was set to star in two other movies, *Last Train from Gun Hill*, a John Sturges western costarring Tony Quinn, and *The Devil's Disciple*, a Revolutionary War story for Burt Lancaster's company. Burt and I would share billing with Sir Laurence Olivier.

Kirk Douglas the actor was doing just fine.

But Kirk Douglas the *businessman* had problems.

My smug self-assurance that Arthur Krim and United Artists would "back my play" on *Spartacus* was instantly deflated when I received this surprising wire from Arthur on January 13:

DEAR KIRK: "SPARTACUS" COVERS THE SAME STORY AS "THE GLADIATORS" BY KOESTLER. WE ARE ALREADY COMMITTED TO "THE GLADIATORS" WITH YUL BRYNNER TO BE DIRECTED BY MARTY RITT WHICH MAKES IT IMPOSSIBLE FOR US TO INTEREST OURSELVES IN "SPARTACUS." BEST—ARTHUR

While I was still reeling from the *Spartacus* news, I went home that night to Anne. She was four months pregnant with our second child, but that hardly explained the growing tension between us.

Anne was the most loving and loyal partner any man could be blessed to have. What she was *not*, however, was naive. She was tough and brutally honest about people, especially about one in particular: Sam Norton. She didn't trust the way he handled my business affairs, even though he was also my best friend. I'd originally met him back in the hallways of Famous Artist Agency, when I was cooling my heels waiting for an audience with the big boss, Charlie Feldman. Sam was a junior guy in the agency, so he had time to shoot the breeze with a young actor. Like me, he was a physical guy—we had both done some wrestling. One day I pinned him to the floor of his office and our friendship was born.

Ten years later, he had become like family to me. I trusted Sam like the brother I never had, like the father I could never count on.

He handled everything—all my personal accounts and investments, as well as the Bryna Company. He got a 10 percent commission on all my deals, and his law firm got big fees for handling my business. I got the peace of mind of never having to worry about money. When I needed anything, Sam sent it to me.

Right from the day we were married, Anne had her doubts about Sam. Minutes before we exchanged vows, he put a prenuptial agreement in front of her and told her to sign it. I explained that Sam was just trying to protect me, but the high-handed way he'd done it had raised Anne's suspicions from that day forward.

Four years later, Anne was not only worried about me, she was concerned about the financial security of our growing family.

"If something happens to you, what happens to us?"

"Anne, for Chrissakes, I've told you a hundred times. Sam will take care of you. He's made me a millionaire. Isn't that enough?!"

Anne looked at me impassively. Her voice was even, but firm. "Kirk, if you're a millionaire, where is all the money? He says you have got so many investments—property, petroleum. Have you ever seen *one* oil well?"

I stormed out of the room. More and more, that was the way these arguments ended. At a deeper level, she was also saying that she didn't trust my judgment. That was hard for me to take.

Back at the office, the news on *Spartacus* went from bad to worse. Marty Ritt, the director of *The Gladiators*, was furious that we were poaching on what he considered *his* historical turf. He told Eddie Lewis that they were way ahead of us with script, location scouting, and casting. Not only did they have Yul Brynner, they'd also signed Tony Quinn. I made a quick call to Tony and he confirmed this was true.

Eddie Lewis and I discussed the possibility of combining the two projects. Marty Ritt would direct. Yul and I would costar. We floated the idea and Marty shot it down quickly: "No way. Yul won't work with Kirk. He hates him."

Marty didn't dare say this to me directly, because it wasn't true.

Yul and I went on to make two pictures together. And, when he and Frank Sinatra were on the outs, Yul came and stayed with me and Anne in Palm Springs. That sure is a funny way to "hate" a guy.

Another surprise. We found out that United Artists had also trademarked several possible names for their *Gladiators* project, including *Spartacus.* Now we owned the rights to a book, but not the title!

There's always been a certain part of my personality that kicks in when people tell me I can't do something. "You *can't* make Spartacus." "You *can't* trust Sam Norton."

I'd had enough of being told "You *can't.*"

The last straw came with an ad in *Daily Variety*—a full-page picture of Yul Brynner looking ferocious in a rented Spartacus costume. "The Gladiators—next from United Artists!" was emblazoned across the photo.

In that moment, I realized they were bluffing. They hadn't shot a frame of film. The word around town was that *The Gladiators* had a budget of $5.5 million. My anger turned to determination.

I called their bluff. I sent Arthur Krim another wire:

ARTHUR: WE ARE SPENDING FIVE MILLION FIVE
HUNDRED AND TWO DOLLARS ON SPARTACUS.
YOUR MOVE, KIRK.

I sent the smart-alecky wire, but I didn't feel so brave. I'm a pretty good actor and I played the role of someone who was confident and sure. But underneath I was afraid and wondered what I was getting myself into.

As I sit here today writing this, I realize I've grown more conservative with age. I don't mean that in a political sense. I mean that I'm less impulsive now, less likely to take a foolhardy risk. When I was making Spartacus, *I was young, reckless. I insisted that I do all my own stunts. Now I have two new knees and a bad back. Was it worth it? With age you think differently.*

Howard Fast began working on the script in New Jersey, and we went around Hollywood looking for a studio.

We were running a race with *The Gladiators*. It felt like they had a chariot with a full team of horses, while I was chasing after them on foot, hoping to keep up.

Everywhere I went, they had been there first. Paramount. MGM. Columbia. Two movies about Spartacus? Forget it. It seemed United Artists' bluff had worked. The race was over and Yul Brynner's picture had won.

I went to see my new agent, Lew Wasserman. Lew was the head of MCA, the most powerful talent agency in Hollywood. Their client list read like a Who's Who of Hollywood—Jimmy Stewart and Henry Fonda, as well as newer stars like Marlon Brando and Marilyn Monroe.

Lew had his own big desk he always kept spotlessly clean— the important information was in his head. Lew Wasserman knew more and forgot less than anyone in Hollywood.

"What's happening with *Spartacus*?" he asked, owlish behind his thick glasses.

"We've been all over town with it, Lew. That damned *Variety* ad makes it seem like *The Gladiators* is in the can. Nobody wants to risk a fight."

Lew was a man of few words. "What about Universal?"

"We haven't been there yet."

Had it come to this? Universal-International Pictures was a studio where you went in desperation. My friend Tony Curtis was under contract there. He couldn't wait to get out. *"Jesus, Kirk. I'm on a lot with Ma and Pa Kettle and Francis the Talking Mule!"*

They were also hemorrhaging money. Could they even *afford* a project of this size? None of this seemed to concern Lew. He rose, signaling the end of our meeting.

"I'll have Eddie Muhl call you."

Ed Muhl was head of production for Universal. Within hours, he called. Lew had wasted no time.

"It's a great book, Kirk. I've read it. But do you think it's a movie?"

"I really do, Ed. We're going to build the whole story around Spartacus the man, not describe him in flashback the way Fast does in the book."

In Fast's novel, Spartacus is dead at the opening of the story. You didn't meet him, you only heard him talked about. And even in flashback, he dies right in the middle of the book.

"Lew tells me Howard Fast is writing the script. Kirk, I'm a little nervous about that."

"Don't worry, Ed. He understands the book won't play dramatically. He'll do what we need."

I wasn't at all sure Fast *could* do it.

"No, no. It's not that. It's the Communist thing. We've got enough headaches over here."

I was surprised. I thought that Fast's public recanting and denunciation of Communism was common knowledge.

"He's no Red. Fast told them all to go to hell. They hate him now."

"*I* know that, Kirk. And *you* know that. But try telling it to Hedda Hopper. That woman has the memory of an elephant."

I laughed. "You mean she has the *legs* of an elephant."

Muhl was laughing too. A good sign. I moved in to try and close the deal. "How about this, Ed? I'll have a first draft of the screenplay in four weeks. If you like it, we take it from there."

"Okay, Kirk. We'll put the word out that we're thinking of making *Spartacus* with Fast. If there's no big reaction, we *might* be able to use him. Get me a script as soon you can."

I quickly called Lew Wasserman. He came on the line without saying hello.

"How did it go with Muhl?"

"I think he might be in, but he's worried about Howard Fast. We need to get him a script in four weeks."

Lew was already moving on. "How do you see it cast?"

I took a deep breath. "What about Larry Olivier, Charles Laughton, and Peter Ustinov?"

Anybody else might have dismissed me as delusional. Not Lew.

"Why not?" was his immediate reply.

"You think we could get them?"

"They're my clients. You sure as hell can *talk* to them."

That night, I told Anne that *Spartacus* might really happen. All we needed now was for Howard Fast to come through with a script.

Unfortunately, he did.

We'd flown Fast out to California from New Jersey, setting him up at the Beverly Hills Hotel. The now-former Communist didn't complain about his posh digs, but he was already showing signs of becoming a major pain in the ass. I should have seen it coming when he asked me if I had optioned *Spartacus* just because his name was so valuable.

Still, Fast was writing steadily. Two weeks after he arrived in California, he sent us his first draft.

"This is crap!" Eddie Lewis said about what Howard Fast had just handed in to us. He got no argument from me.

Dear God, it was awful—sixty pages of lifeless characters uttering leaden speeches. It was as if he hadn't read his own novel. There was no dramatic arc, no spine on which to build a usable script.

"Get Fast in here now!"

"He's busy, Kirk!"

"I want to see him."

"He's giving a lecture over at UCLA."

I'd promised Muhl a screenplay in four weeks. We'd used up half that time with nothing to show for it. Fast hadn't worked for us. Now we needed speed.

I had an idea.

Bryna had another writer, Sam Jackson, who we had just put under contract. He was working on adapting a novel that I really liked, *The Brave Cowboy,* by Edward Abbey. I hadn't met this Jackson fellow yet, but I knew his reputation. He was the quickest writer in Hollywood. I knew something else about him too. Although we had hired him under the name of "Sam Jackson," that was not his real name.

It was Dalton Trumbo. And I didn't give a damn about his politics.

I asked Eddie Lewis to set up a meeting with him right away. There was the obvious problem of where to meet, since no blacklisted writer had set foot on a studio lot in more than a decade, and Dalton Trumbo was a highly recognizable figure. If his trademark handlebar mustache was spotted on the Universal lot, a panicked Eddie Muhl might shut down the whole film.

Trumbo came out to my house, a half-hour's drive from his home near Pasadena. Once the highest-paid writer in the business, he now drove an old car that could barely make the drive over the pass to Beverly Hills.

I opened the door to greet him. He was small, graying. The mustache dwarfed his face, yet his eyes—magnified by thick glasses—were his dominant feature. They had warmth and intelligence, along with a direct quality that said this guy was no phony.

"It's a pleasure to finally meet you, *Sam,*" I said, escorting him into my living room.

"So this is how the other half lives," he said disarmingly.

The rapport between us was instant and easy. Over coffee, I asked him how he had come up with the name "Sam Jackson."

"Did you ever see a movie I wrote called *The Remarkable Andrew?*"

"No, but I loved *Kitty Foyle* and *A Guy Named Joe.*" Then, grinning, I added, "*The Brave One* was a terrific picture too."

He smiled, taking a long drag from the cigarette that he kept perpetually lit in his signature black holder. "Bill Holden plays a young man named Andrew—a bookkeeper framed for a crime he didn't commit. Railroaded off to jail, he's visited by the ghost of General Andrew Jackson. He tells him to fight, that 'one man with courage makes a majority.'

"I wrote that in 1942, before all this blacklist nonsense." He waved his cigarette in the air, dismissively, then added, "The 'Sam' is for Samuel Adams, one of my favorite Founding Fathers."

As we continued to get acquainted, we discovered that we shared the same birthday—December ninth! Trumbo was born in Colorado in 1905. That made him exactly eleven years older than I was, to the day.

I told him that I'd first received *Spartacus* on "our" birthday. He flicked the ashes from his cigarette and said drily, "So where's *my* copy?"

I don't believe in coincidences. I've said that often. Sometimes the universe shows you that you're precisely where you belong, often by putting you together with exactly the right person.

I gave my new friend "Sam" a copy of the book and he promised to read it right away.

I had been thinking a lot about the day when the blacklist would end. No more fronts. No more pseudonyms. The question was not "if" that day would come, but "when."

But I knew I couldn't take that chance with *Spartacus*. With a budget of at least five million, the risk was just too great.

We still hadn't told Howard Fast that his script was unsalvageable. We couldn't afford to. We might need his name on the final version, no matter who wrote it. His insufferable ego notwithstanding, there were Writers Guild issues to be dealt with. We would need a front, even for rewrites. As a producer, Eddie Lewis could play that part without violating Guild rules. That would be the plan.

Complicating things further, Dalton Trumbo and Howard Fast had their own "unfriendly" history. They had only met once, in New York, on the night Trumbo was released from prison.

Here's how he described the single time their paths had crossed. I only wish you could hear his voice:

My wife had just got me out of jail at midnight. . . . We took a B&O to New York and some of the attorneys had a little dinner in an apartment and Howard Fast arrived, and I saw him through the door. I had never met him, but I had heard stories of him from convicts who had transferred from his jail to our jail, and they found him a baffling, wonderful mystery.

I saw him enter from the hall, see me, turn back, and then make a big entrance.

And then he said, "Fellow convict! How are you?!"

And there was something about it that irritated me and I was a little high and I said, "By what right do you call me a fellow convict—what did you serve? Ninety days with time off for good behavior?! You are no convict. You are a little casualty."

He's not a funny man, you know.

Trumbo's humor was his saving grace. And I decided it would be ours as well. Trumbo—"Sam Jackson"—was the only guy who could get us a great script in the short window of time we had left. He was stunningly prolific. Where other top writers could turn out twenty pages per week, he could do twice that amount in one day!

But would he do it? The call came the next day.

He refused to let his feelings about Howard Fast, personal or political, stand in the way: "If I were to turn this down because of the author, because I disagreed with the politics or the public behavior or the private behavior of the author, I would become a party to the same blacklist that I have been dedicating my life to fighting."

He had agreed to adapt the Fast book.

Eddie Lewis and I were elated. I said to him, "Dalton Trumbo. It's too bad we can't use that name. I like the sound of it. 'Trummbbo!' Don't you hear trumpets blaring and drums beating?"

In forty-eight hours Trumbo sent us a seven-step outline based on Fast's novel. The difference was immediately apparent—and brilliant. In two days, he had created the entire character of Spartacus—a slave who starts out as a savage, an animal, then grows into a man with a heart, a brain, a soul. Ultimately, he becomes a leader—a hero to thousands of men.

Eddie Lewis had the unenviable task of presenting this new structure to Howard Fast. Worse yet (for Eddie), he had to claim it as his own.

Predictably, Fast exploded, berating and belittling Eddie as a "half-wit" with delusions of being a genuine writer—like him. It's possible to laugh about it now, but at the time we ran the very real risk of Howard Fast blowing up the whole deal.

After much persuasion—and massive ego massage—Fast agreed to continue writing *his* screenplay based on the "Lewis" outline. We knew that his work would never be used. He never had a clue about the parallel play that was being written simultaneously by "Sam Jackson."

For the next two weeks, Dalton worked almost around the clock to produce the script that we would actually send to Universal.

Trying to spare both his time and the wear and tear on his old car, I made the trip out to his house several times during that frenetic fortnight.

I'd often find him working in the bathtub. He had a wooden tray set across the top, which preserved his modesty and gave him a place to put his typewriter, an ashtray, and an ever-present glass of bourbon.

He was a unique, idiosyncratic guy who, like me, loved animals. He was particularly fond of birds, often rescuing injured ones and nursing them back to health. He had so many parakeets and mockingbirds that he built an aviary for them in his backyard.

One bird he didn't have—and always wanted—was a parrot. So I bought him one. He bonded with that bird. It was often perched on his shoulder while he was writing in the tub.

My other friend Sam—Norton—told me I could deduct the

parrot later as a business expense. When I laughingly told this to Anne, she just rolled her eyes—more of Sam's creative "advice."

Universal loved the "Eddie Lewis" draft. We got a tentative green light from Muhl. But we still needed a major star to win the race with United Artists and Yul Brynner.

Laurence Olivier was the greatest actor in the English-speaking world. He remained at the top of our list. We'd heard (from Lew Wasserman) that United Artists intended to send Olivier the *Gladiators* script as soon as it was ready.

There, I had a slight advantage. Burt Lancaster and I were coproducing a film called *The Devil's Disciple*, costarring Olivier. I would be spending the summer with Larry in London.

The Gladiators had a top director in Marty Ritt. Lew Wasserman felt strongly that in order to nail down the deal with Universal, we needed to lock in a good director. Quickly.

Eddie Lewis and I went through our Rolodex of possibilities. The first one we came to was a "D," Delmer Daves. He'd done *Demetrius and the Gladiators*, but he had heart problems and couldn't commit to a major project.

We kept looking. "E." "F." "G." Eddie liked the British director Peter Glenville. No go—he had a play on Broadway.

"K." Stanley Kubrick. *Paths of Glory* had been a critical success. However, as I'd predicted, it made no money. (It hadn't helped that the French and German governments had done everything they could to kill it, short of burning the prints.) Besides, Kubrick was in preproduction to direct a Brando film called *One-Eyed Jacks*.

I spun the Rolodex. "L." David Lean. Perfect! He'd just won the Academy Award for Best Director with *Bridge on the River Kwai*.

We got the draft script to him immediately. He was equally as quick in politely passing on our offer: "I can't somehow fit myself into it style-wise. I couldn't bring it off. Best of luck to you!" (I learned later that Lean had his heart set on an even bigger project, adapting the T. E. Lawrence novel *Seven Pillars of Wisdom*. Four years later he succeeded on a grand scale—*Lawrence of Ara-*

bia. Passing on *Spartacus* was a good move for Lean, if not for us.) We were at the "M"s. Joe Mankiewicz! Now *there* was an idea. He'd done *Julius Caesar,* and we had worked well together on *A Letter to Three Wives.* He had just finished writing and directing *The Quiet American* with Audie Murphy. Joe had nothing on his plate.

I called Lew Wasserman. No pleasantries, just a quick, "No, Kirk. With a budget this big, Universal wants a technician they can manage. That's not Joe."

Damn, we hadn't even made the final deal with Universal and they were already sticking their camel's nose deep into *my* tent. This was not a good sign. I reluctantly went back to the Rolodex.

Where was I? Oh yeah, "M." I skipped right past Anthony Mann. He was a good director but not right for *Spartacus.* He'd done a lot of westerns. But *Spartacus* was not going to be a Roman-style western. I had no interest in doing a "shoot 'em up" with spears.

Halfway through the alphabet and we were striking out big-time. I paused. "Olivier." Should I ask him to play a major part *and* direct? Would that be an incentive or would it make it even less likely that he'd agree? I took out his card and set it aside.

I finished turning the wheel of names. George Stevens was unavailable. Willy Wyler was shooting *Ben-Hur.* He had *his* epic.

Nobody! I called Lew Wasserman back. He encouraged me to talk with Olivier about directing while I was with him in London. He also said that Universal really liked Anthony Mann, as did he. Mann was a technician. Not an artist. Not a perfectionist. He was the kind of guy the studios loved because he could keep a picture on schedule and bring it in on budget.

I was surprised. Not about Mann, but by what Lew seemed to know about the inner workings of Universal. I had the sense that he was plugged in there more closely than to any other studio in town. Hell, if that was true, it would be *great* for *Spartacus.* And that was all I cared about. I mean, to make this picture I was willing to be as ruthless and pragmatic as I had to be.

Filming The Devil's Disciple *in London with Laurence Olivier and Burt Lancaster. My other mission was to recruit Olivier for* Spartacus.

CHAPTER FOUR

"I know nothing—nothing. . . . I want to know . . . everything.
Why a star falls and a bird doesn't. Where the sun
goes at night. Why the moon changes shape.
I want to know where the wind comes from . . ."

—Kirk Douglas as Spartacus

Over the years, I've often heard myself repeating those lines aloud
from memory—some of the most beautiful words I've ever spoken
as an actor. Spartacus, the illiterate slave, wondering about the
mysteries of life. There is so much left to know.

"Goddamn it!" I threw down the newspaper. Coffee spilled on
the headline, "Producer Mike Todd Dies in Plane Crash." It was
Monday, March 24, 1958. Mike's private plane had gone down
two days before, en route to New York. I was still numb from the
news. Seeing it in print made it real again—a painful reminder
that it wasn't all a bad dream.

I was supposed to be on that flight. Mike Todd had really pressured me to go with him. As an added inducement, he'd even offered me a stop in Independence, Missouri, to meet former President Harry Truman.

Only Anne's near-mystical insistence that I shouldn't make the trip had kept me from going. We'd fought about it bitterly. Then the bulletin came over the radio while we were out driving. Mike's plane—*Lucky Liz*—had crashed near a small town in New Mexico. I pulled the car over. Anne took my hand and we sat there, both of us weeping.

Elizabeth Taylor was a widow at twenty-six. Thank God, Anne was not.

Thanks to her, I was still alive to face the myriad problems of my *Spartacus* script. True to his reputation, Trumbo (a.k.a. "Sam Jackson") was turning out dazzling pages of dialogue at a phenomenal rate. His prose was like poetry. The pages were so good that it took me several days to notice that he was writing virtually *all* dialogue. Where was the rest of the script?! Then, this note from him clipped to the last page:

> I know you are gravely alarmed, but there's no need to be. The only way I can write a script is from beginning to end, dialogue only. Then I make first corrections. Then I do the script—that is, fill in shots and description and action.

I turned my attention back to the real problem—locking in a winning cast that would defeat *The Gladiators*. Ira Wolfert was writing UA's script. He had only one screenplay to his credit—and he'd done it ten years earlier. Surely he couldn't beat "Sam Jackson" for speed or style in a writers' race.

So I thought, until Eddie Lewis delivered more bad news. Not tragic news on the level of Mike Todd, but information that did not bode well for *Spartacus* vs. *The Gladiators*.

"Wolfert's a front."

"What?"

"He's *their* 'Sam Jackson.'"

"Who's the real writer?"

"Abe Polonsky."

Abe Polonsky was a blacklisted writer/director with a keen mind and a quick pen.

"So, where does that leave us?"

"Fucked!" said Eddie, brightly.

I stood up and started pacing. "If they've got Polonsky, they'll get their script to the Englishmen at least as quickly as we can."

"And they've already got location scouts in Europe."

Europe? I thought about this for a second; then my mood brightened considerably.

"You know what that means, don't you?" I stopped pacing and was grinning at Eddie.

Eddie looked at me blankly.

"Don't you get it? We've got them beat! If they're shooting in Europe, the weather will delay production for at least a year, until late spring or summer. *We* can start in January, right here in the States."

I went on, "We need to have a finished draft by the time I leave for England in July. I want to hand it directly to Olivier along with the Fast book."

Eddie turned to leave.

"Oh," I said, "there's one more thing. Tell 'Sam' he should spend the bulk of his time on the Roman parts. Really flesh them out. I don't care if I get short shrift in the first draft."

Eddie couldn't resist. "Yeah, we already *know* who's playing Spartacus. *He* won't care if he doesn't have any lines."

"Get the hell out of here!" The day had started out so badly, but I was actually beginning to feel a little better.

The next few months flew by. I did a picture for Paramount in Arizona called *Last Train from Gun Hill*. Bryna produced it, along with Hal Wallis' company.

Now the circle was really complete. A dozen years after he gave me my first job in motion pictures, here I was—Issur Danielovitch from Amsterdam, New York—coproducing with Hal Wallis! It was a long way from that first limousine ride through those big Paramount gates.

Tony Quinn costarred in *Last Train*, and although our rival Roman movies were locked in competition, we got along well. Maybe he was keeping his options open for a part in *Spartacus*, just in case *The Gladiators* didn't get off the ground.

I returned to Los Angeles and my very pregnant wife. Our baby was due in four weeks, just before *The Devil's Disciple* would begin shooting in London. Anne was still unconvinced that Sam Norton could be trusted with our financial security, but our arguments had subsided. I was grateful that we were not fighting, particularly now.

Dalton had followed my instructions with respect to the Roman parts. In fact, taking a device from the Fast book, he had opened the script with General Crassus—the character we wanted Olivier to play—describing his battles with Spartacus. The flashback would allow Olivier to tell the story from his character's point of view, thus increasing its importance dramatically. Brilliant!

The other key parts were equally well developed: Trumbo had transformed the Roman senator Gracchus into a character worthy of Charles Laughton, whom we hoped would portray him, and, in Dalton's hand, the unctuous Batiatus, owner of the gladiator school, had become a perfect role for Peter Ustinov.

I was so excited by our progress that I called Lew Wasserman to tell him, privately, that Sam Jackson was really Dalton Trumbo. In life, you never lie to your doctor or your lawyer. In Hollywood, you don't lie to your agent. He does that for you.

I shouldn't have been surprised by Lew's reaction, but I was.

"I know that, Kirk."

"You do? How . . ." I was suddenly worried that all our elaborate precautions to keep Dalton's identity a secret were for naught. Was there a leak? This could kill *Spartacus* in the crib. Hedda Hopper would have a field day, and Universal would pull out before we had a deal.

"Don't worry. Universal doesn't know. Muhl really thinks Eddie Lewis is writing it with Fast."

I had no choice except to trust Lew's judgment. Still, there was a nagging fear in my gut that we would need to deal with this issue sooner or later. I just hoped it would be *much* later— after the picture was released.

Eric Anthony Douglas was born on June 21, 1958. It was a Saturday, the Jewish Sabbath. Anne and I were blessed with our second son.

Ten days later I left for London. The first draft of the *Spartacus* script was still a few months from completion, so I made sure to pack a copy of the Fast novel to give to Olivier. I hoped it would whet his appetite for the part of Crassus.

Based on a play by George Bernard Shaw, *The Devil's Disciple* was a Revolutionary War drama set in New England, yet we were filming it in Old England. When Burt Lancaster and I arrived on the set, Olivier seemed distant, distracted. He wrote about it candidly in his autobiography:

> I was irritatingly not "with it." I gave way to the unattractive habit of getting everyone's names mixed up; the least fortunate of these mistakes was always with Burt—the boss for God's sake! Every time I addressed him as Kirk, he would look at me straight and steely-steady and say quietly, "Burt." I could only stammer that I was afraid I must be having a nervous breakdown. I have thought ever since that my excuse must have been very close to the truth.

I soon learned the reason for Larry's extreme distress: Lady Olivier—Vivien Leigh. Shortly after production began, she hosted a luncheon for Burt and me at their home in Notley. The guests included the urbane George Sanders and his wife, Benita. The Oliviers seemed the picture of gracious hosts.

Suddenly, that image was violently shattered. Vivien, who had been in a private conversation with her husband, raised her voice loud enough to be heard by the entire room. "Larry, why don't you fuck me anymore?"

All conversation stopped. The pain on Larry's face was evident, yet he said nothing. George Sanders broke the tension by raising his wineglass in a mock salute to the couple. "Oh, Vivien, stop," he said sardonically. "In a moment, Benita will be asking the same question and then we're all in for trouble!" Nervous laughter, then talk quietly resumed. Everyone tried not to look at Larry and Vivien.

Moments later, Vivien walked over to me. Her beautiful Scarlett O'Hara eyes were boring directly into mine. In a sultry voice she asked, "Why don't *you* fuck me?"

I couldn't believe what I was hearing. Larry rushed to her side. Even in the midst of this bizarre and uncomfortable scene, his compassion for his wife was evident. Taking her elbow gently, he guided her from the room. I was relieved to be out of the line of fire.

Months later, Larry told me that he reached his breaking point with Vivien soon after that incident. Exhausted from a particularly vicious quarrel that lasted almost until dawn, he grabbed her, dragged her down the hall, and threw her into the bedroom. She struck her head on a table, opening up a bad cut near her eye. Larry said that was the moment he realized if they stayed together any longer, he might kill her—or she him.

At the time, I knew nothing of the malady called bipolar disorder. Nobody did. Now I understand what the Oliviers were coping with because I had a similar experience with my son Eric. He eventually died from this terrible disease. So many people still don't recognize it as an illness. They focus only on the symptoms—the drinking, the dope, the flagrant sexuality. They blame the victim. I've closed my eyes. I'm trying to erase the image of that sad, tortured woman and replace it with the beautiful southern girl that we all fell in love with in Gone with the Wind. *That's how I want to remember her.*

Now I knew why Larry seemed so preoccupied on the set. How could I approach him about *Spartacus* when his personal life was in such turmoil? I held off giving him the book.

A few weeks later, he gave me an opening. "Kirk, there's an annual charity event, 'Night of 100 Stars,' at the London Palladium. I have been asked to organize the entertainment for the evening. Might you and Burt consider performing? It would certainly be a great favor to me."

"Let me talk with Burt. I'm sure we can put something together."

"That's very kind of you. I'm in your debt, sir."

I walked back to my dressing room, smiling. Perfect—this was the time to give him the book.

Olivier read the Fast novel. He was plainly intrigued by the idea of turning it into a film. I broached the prospect of him directing it. He was startled, but quite receptive. He recognized that it would be a tremendous undertaking, but the more we talked about it, the more enthusiastic he became.

Then it was my turn to be startled.

"After my experience with *The Prince and the Showgirl*, I swore I would never direct and star in the same film again. But this . . . *this* would be an extraordinary challenge. This character of Spartacus has so many possibilities!"

He wanted to play Spartacus. I hadn't seen that coming.

My mind was reeling, but Larry was still speaking.

"How soon can I see a draft of the script that your Eddie Lewis is writing?"

"I'll have it before we wrap."

"Good, good." Larry was transforming before my eyes. The withdrawn, unhappy man of the last few weeks was now engaged, excited. How could I tell him that *I* was Spartacus?

I decided to wait. If the part of Crassus continued to expand—and that was Dalton's charge—I hoped Larry would be attracted to it on his own.

The night of July 24, 1958, was definitely one to remember. Burt and I joined Larry and Viv, Noel Coward, Shirley Bassey, Terry Thomas, and dozens of others onstage at the Palladium. As the two guys from across the pond, Burt and I played to the crowd. Donning bowler hats, we entered from opposite sides of the stage, singing "Maybe It's Because I'm a Londoner (That I Love London So)." It brought down the house. Larry loved it.

Even better, he loved the *Spartacus* script that Eddie Lewis brought with him ten days later. Olivier heaped praise on his "brilliant work."

"It's one of the most skillful first drafts I've ever read. It has vitality, scope, seriousness of purpose," Larry effused.

Eddie squirmed. He hated taking credit for something he didn't write.

I squirmed when Larry suggested that I play Crassus. He talked about his vision for the character of Spartacus. Larry felt that the role was developing in a different direction than he had envisioned from the Fast novel. He was right, of course. That's exactly what we'd intended when we rejected Howard's pages. We knew the saintlike father figure from the novel would never play on-screen. The human qualities of a slave who falls in love with a woman, and then with his freedom—those were the essential elements of the story.

If Larry didn't see it our way, maybe he would still change his mind about which part he wanted to play. Then we'd have the best of both worlds: Olivier directing *himself* as General Crassus.

We left him with the promise of a second draft of the script and turned our attention to Charles Laughton.

He was appearing in a production of *The Party* at the New Theatre in London's West End. Eddie and I went to visit him backstage. We'd already sent him the script.

I'd never met Laughton. I was a little nervous about it. Long before I became an actor, I wrote him the only fan letter I've ever sent anybody. His stunning performance as Quasimodo in *The Hunchback of Notre Dame* moved me deeply. I was mesmerized by Laughton's ability to seemingly change himself into a different person on-screen.

What I didn't know about Charles Laughton was that his amazing gift was also his curse. His talent allowed him to lose himself completely in a role, yet it left him extremely vulnerable when he *wasn't* acting. He protected himself with a diffidence that bordered on rudeness. Anger was his armor.

If I had any illusions about meeting my childhood idol, they disappeared moments after Eddie and I entered his dressing room.

Sitting in an overstuffed chair, Laughton didn't rise to greet us. He took my hand like an offering. He motioned toward the *Spartacus* script.

"Mr. Douglas," he declared imperiously, "this is shit." He waved his hand dismissively. "I'm not interested."

It went downhill from there. It was obvious that he hadn't even read the script. Somehow he had divined that it wasn't worthy of him.

"Olivier likes it. He wants to direct it," I said.

"That would be a *disaster*," said Laughton, his elegant voice drawing out the word. "You must understand that Larry is simply not capable of a project like this."

We stood there like schoolboys called before the headmaster. There was no further opportunity for discussion. We could only listen as he repeated himself for emphasis: "Simply not capable. A disaster."

Class ended. We were dismissed from Laughton's room.

On the street, Eddie and I just stared at each other for a moment, still stunned from the Laughton "treatment."

I spoke first. "Well, that couldn't have gone any worse."

"At least Sir Laurence thinks I'm brilliant," said Eddie, wryly.

"Yeah, but Laughton agrees with Fast that you're a lousy writer."

Laughing, we went off in search of the nearest pub.

The next day I called Lew Wasserman in Los Angeles to tell him that Olivier wanted my part and Laughton wanted nothing to do with the project.

He was, as always, unsurprised. "Larry is interested. Give him time. Laughton needs the money. He will do it."

"But, Lew . . ." I began.

He cut me off. "Call Ustinov in Switzerland. Let me know after you've spoken with him." He hung up.

I placed a person-to-person call to Mr. Peter Ustinov in Switzerland. A few minutes later the operator rang me back. "Mr. Douglas, I have Mr. Ustinov on the line."

"Kirk!" His ebullient voice crackled through the wire.

"Hello, Peter!" I shouted to be heard through the static. "Did you get the script?"

"I did. I was quite taken with this Eddie Lewis you have working for you. He's a talented writer." That was two votes for Eddie. Now it was a split decision.

"What do you think of the part?"

"Well, it's certainly very different from *Quo Vadis*, but I think my toga still fits."

"That's wonderful, Peter! I think it's a great part for you."

"I'm honored to be considered for it, Kirk."

Within the hour, Lew Wasserman called with an update. "Laughton's in. So is Peter."

I couldn't believe it. Lew had been exactly right about Laughton. "So, if Olivier says yes, then we have a green light from Universal?" "Yes," said Wasserman, succinct as ever.

Flying back to California, I read a memo from Sam Norton. *The Vikings* was breaking box office records in theaters across the country. We had a hit! According to Sam, Bryna's $4 million investment would be recouped more than threefold in the United States alone.

Riding home from the airport, my mood was upbeat. After two months of dreary English weather, it was good to be home. I was eager to see Anne, Peter, and the new baby, Eric. I missed my family.

I walked through the front door yelling, "Anne!" She didn't answer. That was strange; she knew when I was due home. I walked into the living room and saw her sitting alone on the couch. There were some papers on her lap.

She didn't come over to greet me. In fact, she didn't even look up.

"Honey, where's the baby? What's wrong?" Suddenly, I was alarmed.

"The baby's fine. He's sleeping." Her voice was quiet.

"Then what is it? I'm gone for two months and you can't even get up off the couch to kiss me?"

"I have something to tell you." Something in her tone stopped me cold.

"Kirk, sit down."

My mind was racing. What was going on here? Had I done something wrong? Were those *divorce* papers on her lap? This couldn't be happening. I sat down in a chair facing her and waited for her to speak.

She looked up at me and said, "I tried to tell you, but you wouldn't listen."

"Tell me what?"

"Your friend Sam Norton is a crook. He's been robbing you blind."

"Now, Anne . . ."

She cut me off sharply.

"Kirk, I have the proof! I had Price-Waterhouse look at all the books. He's a fraud. There's no money."

"You hired an accountant behind my back? How could you do that?"

"Because you wouldn't believe me." She said it so softly I could barely hear her. She was looking down again at the papers in her lap. I could tell she was crying.

"Honey . . ." I got up, sat down beside her, and put my arm around her shoulder, pulling her close. Anne was trembling. The papers fell from her lap onto the floor.

I reached down to pick them up and saw the cover sheet. It was the summary of an audit. I saw the names "Mr. Kirk Douglas" and "Brynaprod, S.A.," the legal name of my company.

As Anne watched silently, I began looking through the report. This *couldn't* be true. I had no money? I owed huge amounts to the government in unpaid taxes?!

I was dumbfounded. I looked at Anne. "My best friend, he was like my father. . . . You were right. I was an idiot. He played me like a violin. I'm gonna kill him!" I started back toward the door, the audit clutched in my hand like a weapon.

I turned around. "You were right about him all along!"

"Darling, anger won't solve anything."

"So what am I supposed to do? Just take it? Let him fuck me? Let him steal from us?" Now *I* had tears in my eyes. The betrayal, the sense of helplessness—it was all hitting me at once.

I stood there in the middle of the room, staring at my wife. She came over and put her arms around me. She held on for a long time.

Finally, she said, "Let's fix you some scrambled eggs and I'll tell you what the accountant thinks we can do. It's bad, but it may not be as bad as it looks." She smiled now, just a bit.

I looked at her. What a wonderful girl. Anne had saved my life once because I listened to her and didn't get into that airplane.

If I'd done that when she'd first warned me about Sam Norton, maybe I—*we*—wouldn't be in this fix now.

I smiled back at her. "I'm starving. Let's eat." I followed her into the kitchen.

In the days that followed, Anne and I met with a battery of accountants and attorneys. Their plan was a smart one. Instead of beating up Sam, I'd play him like he'd played me. I'd go to him with the audit and say that I knew he wasn't capable of such duplicity. He must have been duped by his partner, Jerry Rosenthal. I'd convince Sam that I still trusted *him*. I would ask Sam to leave his partner and became president of my company. All he'd have to do was sign some papers that revoked their firm's power of attorney over my finances.

It was the performance of my career. It took all my self-control not to dangle him by the ankles out of his office window. Greatly relieved that I wasn't blaming him, Sam Norton bought the whole pitch. He signed on the spot. I left him behind his big desk—the desk I'd paid for—convinced that he'd hear from me shortly about moving over to Bryna to oversee *Spartacus*.

We never spoke again.

Fortunately, the tremendous success of *The Vikings* helped soften the blow of Sam Norton's thievery. I could pay back what I owed the government, but I was still effectively broke. That meant *Spartacus* was an even bigger risk than I thought. Should I just back away before I got in too deep?

I got a call from Vernon Scott, the respected Hollywood reporter for United Press International. He wanted to talk about my plans for a follow-up to *The Vikings*. I didn't hesitate.

"At the end of this year I'm starting production on *Spartacus*—

about the uprising of the Roman slaves. It will be bigger and more expensive than *The Vikings*. If you aren't going ahead in this business, you're sliding back. And I'm willing to gamble, rather than slide."

I still hadn't heard from Olivier. Then, in mid-September, this letter arrived:

> I have now contracted myself to go to Stratford-on-Avon for the fourth play of the season next year, which is "Coriolanus," and to start rehearsing in June. I imagine this decision will fairly knock me out for any further consideration as director of the film. If, however, you can still see your way to improving the part of Crassus in relation to the other three roles, then I should be more than happy to look at it again as it is such a gallant enterprise and one I should be extremely proud to be part of. Could you be so kind as to let me see something just as soon as you possibly can?

Charles Laughton, Peter Ustinov, and now Laurence Olivier! All three had signed on *and* I was now free to play Spartacus without offending Larry. Yul Brynner and *The Gladiators* were all but history.

The only thing *The Gladiators* had that we didn't have was a director, Marty Ritt.

Ritt and I ran into each other at the annual meeting of production heads and distributors in Miami. Each studio would be announcing its slate of films for 1959.

Marty cornered me in the lobby of the Fontainebleau Hotel. He knew we'd secured Olivier, Laughton, and Ustinov for *Spartacus* because he'd been chasing them too.

"Kirk, what do you say we join forces?"

"That ship has sailed, Marty."

"But United Artists owns the name 'Spartacus,' you know that."

He was right. Our lawyers had been working on it, but the

Motion Picture Association's Title Registration Bureau had ruled in United Artists' favor.

"Marty, let's just see what happens."

Inside, the studio chiefs were seated around the conference table in alphabetical order, so "Universal" was up last, immediately following "United Artists."

Arthur Krim, speaking on behalf of UA, announced *The Gladiators*, a film starring Yul Brynner based on the Roman slave revolt led by Spartacus. Then Milton Rackmil, president of Universal International Pictures, said, "Universal will begin production in January on *Spartacus*, a story of the Roman slave revolt starring Kirk Douglas."

The room erupted in laughter. Even Krim and Rackmil were laughing. Game on.

When the meeting adjourned, I walked over to Krim.

"Arthur, we've done pretty well with *The Vikings*, haven't we? And we're going to be doing business together for a long time. Maybe not on this picture, but there'll be plenty more down the road. Let's not let a stupid title get in the way of that."

Arthur was silent for a moment. "Let me get back to New York and talk to our people. Have a safe flight home, Kirk. Give my love to Anne."

"You too, Arthur. And mine to your new bride." Arthur had just married a brilliant Swiss doctor named Mathilde (who would later become a pioneer in AIDS research).

A telegram from United Artists was waiting for me when I got home:

DEAR KIRK - AT ARTHURS REQUEST YUL BRYNNER HAS AGREED IN THE INTERESTS OF GOOD WILL TO YOUR USE OF TITLE "SPARTACUS."

The white flag. *The Gladiators* had surrendered. Now all we needed was a director.

New discovery Sabina Bethman and the cast of Spartacus

CHAPTER FIVE

*"Singer of songs . . . that's my work. I also juggle.
I can do feats of magic."*

—Tony Curtis as Antoninus

DESPITE THE ODDS, WE'D WON our race with *The Gladiators*. But the victory was not without cost. *Spartacus* was now careening into production without a director, a leading lady, or a finished script.

Actually, we had too many scripts. Dalton Trumbo (still known on the leather-bound script covers as "Sam Jackson") would later say he generated a quarter of a million words in the course of writing *Spartacus*. Many thousands of these came in the form of the multicolored pages that had expanded and deepened the roles of the English actors—Sir Laurence Olivier, Charles Laughton, and Peter Ustinov. Their parts were now central to the film. That would come back to haunt us when we started shooting.

Our start date was now three months away. My immediate problem remained finding a strong director. With Olivier out of the running (which came as a great relief to Laughton), we were back to square one.

I briefly considered Marty Ritt. It would be a consolation prize of sorts after he lost out on *The Gladiators*. Not available. He and Yul Brynner were still finishing their screen version of William Faulkner's *The Sound and the Fury*.

With each passing day, Universal was growing more excited about the prospects for *Spartacus*. At a budget of $4 million, this was by far the biggest picture on their production schedule. Their future was on the line with this picture, not to mention mine. The rumors of the studio's insolvency (and its possible sale) were swirling around the lot. Decca Records, which owned Universal, denied them repeatedly. In Hollywood, that often serves as confirmation.

Lew Wasserman remained the patron saint of *Spartacus*. Without his sage counsel and powers of persuasion, we wouldn't have a cast or a studio. Now I needed his help again.

In early November of 1958, I went to see him. Surprisingly, Lew was uncharacteristically expansive. Never one for small talk, he casually asked me how I was getting along with "the boys at Universal." There was an odd look on his face, an almost devilish glint in his eye. This wasn't like him at all.

"Ed Muhl is calling me every day, Lew. He's my new best friend."

It was true. Now that he had given us the green light, Universal's production chief was taking a hands-on role with *Spartacus*. So far, it was a good working relationship. They were going out of their way to accommodate me and my entire team.

"That's good." Lew was smiling. He knew something that he wasn't telling me.

"Is there something happening with Universal that I should know about?"

I wouldn't have believed it possible, but Lew was actually beaming.

"Kirk, can you keep a secret?"

"Lew, you know I can."

He cleared his throat. "Next month, MCA is going to buy the entire Universal lot—367 acres, the soundstages, all the offices—everything but the studio itself."

I whistled. So *that* was why Lew seemed to know so much about the inner workings of Universal. He was buying the lot! My agent was about to become my landlord.

"That's terrific!" I extended my hand. "Congratulations!"

He shook it. "Thank you, Kirk."

Then, Lew's smile instantly disappeared. Once again—all business.

"We need to find you a director. Muhl wants Anthony Mann."

"Anthony Mann?!"

"Kirk . . . I agree."

"Jesus, I don't know, Lew. Do you really think he's up to it?"

"I do. And Universal does. Trust me on this. He's good."

I swallowed hard. I didn't think he was the right director, but a bird in the hand . . . ? "Okay, it's Mann."

As I drove back to my office, I mentally ran through the *Spartacus* list: studio, check; director, check; Olivier, Laughton, Ustinov—check, check, and check. It had taken us eight months of hard work and strategy to defeat *The Gladiators*, but we did it. Checkmate.

As I pulled into my parking space, I couldn't shake the worrisome feeling that we'd won the battle but might still lose the war.

In order to preempt the competition, we were now locked in to a late-January start date. Location scouts were already in Death Valley looking for a barren stretch of sand and rock to replicate the Libyan desert, where the Thracian slave Spartacus was captured and sold to the owner of the gladiator school to be trained for the amusement of his Roman masters.

This crucial scene would eventually start the picture, but Olivier still believed that his character, General Crassus, would open the film with a narrative description of Spartacus' emergence as the leader of the slave revolt. This flashback device had persuaded Larry to play the part.

I knew that we weren't committed to doing it that way. Olivier did not.

The unfinished script was the chief dilemma facing our new director, Tony Mann. My biggest problem was the one major casting decision left to be made: the female lead, Varinia, a slave girl who falls in love with Spartacus.

To me, it was important that this girl should have an accent that was distinctly different from the patrician Romans, and those parts were all being played by British actors.

As a favor, I did test one American actress, my old girlfriend Gene Tierney. I felt sorry for her. Like Vivien Leigh, Gene suffered from severe mental health problems. Two years earlier, after numerous electric shock treatments failed to cure her chronic depression, she walked out on a building ledge, ready to jump. Rescued at the last minute by police, she was hospitalized again for many months. Slowly, she improved. Even before I saw the footage, I could tell she wasn't right anymore. Gene— the beautiful girl I once dated, the actress who captivated movie audiences as "Laura"—was gone. The spark in her eyes just wasn't there anymore.

My first serious choice was a stunning blond French girl, Jeanne Moreau. Her smoldering sexuality and deeply expressive eyes evoked a young Bette Davis (a comparison that she later told me she hated—"I can't *stand* Bette Davis").

Jeanne's recent film with director Louis Malle, *The Lovers*, was garnering international attention. Her performance as a young married woman who abandons her family after a casual sexual affair was suggestive to the point of controversy. The film was banned in parts of America for its "obscenity."

A theater owner in Cleveland was convicted of obscenity for showing *The Lovers*. The case went all the way up to the Supreme Court, which eventually threw out his sentence. This led Justice Potter Stewart to make his famous statement about pornography: "I know it when I see it, and the motion picture involved in this case is not that."

In the prefeminist 1950s, few actresses would take a risk like that. That's why I thought Moreau would be perfect for the role of a slave girl who's literally liberated from a life of indentured servitude.

When I went to see Jeanne in Paris, she was in a play, *La Bonne Soupe*, at the Théâtre du Gymnase. I took her out for dinner. She was even more beautiful in person than on-screen.

I offered to buy out the run of the play if she would come to America and portray Varinia. I told her she would become the biggest star in the world. None of this mattered to her. Politely, Jeanne turned me down cold.

I was disappointed. Orson Welles subsequently called Jeanne Moreau "the greatest actress in the world"—but she was not going to prove it in *Spartacus*. I still needed a leading lady.

Somehow, Jean Simmons got a copy of the script and was badgering me to play Varinia. She was living on a ranch in Arizona with her husband, Stewart Granger. I had great respect for Jean, a beautiful girl and lovely actress, but she was British—that just wasn't the accent I wanted.

MCA sent the script to Ingrid Bergman, who I didn't think was right for the part. Fortunately, she didn't like the story, calling it "too bloody."

Elsa Martinelli, my "fan" from *20,000 Leagues Under the Sea*, was no longer under contract to my company. She'd wanted the freedom to do other pictures, so I let her go as she'd asked—and now her career was floundering. She was back in Italy making low-budget films.

I've never stood in the way of someone's career. A contract is just a piece of paper. If it doesn't represent an artist's true commitment, no amount of money can make up for that.

If Elsa had stayed under contract to Bryna, I probably would have given her the part. Unfortunately—for both of us—she was no longer a credible choice.

We were under the gun. As Thanksgiving approached, we decided to put out a worldwide casting call. If an established actress wasn't available, why not a newcomer? It would be a funny story—*"Slave girl wanted for $5 million picture; no experience necessary."* The columnists would love it, and we'd get a lot of free publicity out of the search itself.

Eddie Lewis and I looked at reel after reel of beautiful young European women. My eyes were bleary and I went home.

Anne wasn't sympathetic to my "plight." She just looked up from dinner and said, "I thought you wanted a good actress. What does it matter where she comes from, so long as she can act?"

"Jesus, Anne! How many times do I have to tell you that Varinia can't speak with a British or American accent?!"

Wiping the corner of her mouth with a napkin, she held my gaze steadily. I knew that look. "Then why did you do a screen test with your old girlfriend Gene Tierney?"

"How did you even know about her?" Anne had a third eye when it came to the women in my life.

She folded the napkin back into her lap and continued eating. "I know a lot about you, Mr. Douglas," she said, her blue eyes twinkling.

Finally, we found the right girl. She was a twenty-seven-year-old German beauty named Sabine Bethmann. The screen test captured her incandescence—a breathtaking, almost ethereal loveliness. Her blond hair and blue eyes would be striking in Technirama, the new wide-screen format we'd decided to use for *Spartacus*.

She looked even younger than her twenty-seven years. This, too, was an important asset. The character of Varinia, a girl who falls in love with Spartacus, must be able to convey the innocence and optimism of youth. Sabine Bethmann, on camera, had that quality. Eddie and I looked at each other in relief.

There was still a huge amount of preparation we had to do, just to get her ready for the part. The problem was she barely spoke any English. Her short film experience was entirely in the German cinema. She would be very difficult for American audiences to understand. We hired the best coach available, Jeff Corey, a blacklisted actor who, out of necessity, had become a respected drama teacher.

Universal's publicity department created a whole campaign around our new "star." They started by changing the spelling of her name, replacing an "e" with an "a" and dropping an "n." Sabine Bethmann became "Sabina Bethman." In a town filled with Tabs, Troys, and Rocks, I'm sure someone thought this was a brilliant idea.

In the middle of all this, my friend Bernie Schwartz called— he had also changed his name . . . to "Tony Curtis."

"How's it going, Big Panther?"

I laughed. Tony once told a reporter that I was like a panther with a thorn in his side, muscles taut, prowling the set. In those days, it was true.

"Tony! How's Janet?

"She's doing great. Big as a house. The baby is due any minute." Tony and Janet Leigh already had a young daughter about Peter's age—Kelly. The new baby would be named Jamie Lee.

"That's great! Tell her that Anne and I send our love."

"I will. I will." A pause. "So, when do you start shooting *Spartacus*?"

"In two months. We just found this beautiful German girl for the lead."

A longer pause.

"Hey, Tony, what's the matter?"

"I'm kind of hurt there's no part in it for me. Don't you love me anymore?"

That was all I needed right now—friends hitting me up to be in a picture that didn't even have a finished script.

"Are you schnorring me, you sonofabitch?" I deliberately used the Yiddish word, which means wheedling a person until he gives you something for free. I wasn't angry, just annoyed by his brashness. But that was Tony. He could be very persistent.

"Kirk, boychick, it doesn't have to be a big part. A couple of scenes will be enough to get rid of one of my commitments to Universal."

I knew Tony hated working at Universal. *Spartacus* would put him one step closer to getting out of his contract.

"I started at Universal when I was nothing and they still treat me like nothing." Tony's voice was filled with anger.

I understood. The same thing happened to me when I started in the business with producer Hal Wallis. When I refused to sign a seven-picture contract extension with him, he threatened to drop me. I said, "Fuck you. Then drop me!" I pulled the thorn out of my own side.

"Tony, I can't think of any part that would be right for you."

There *was* a small, but crucial, role: that of another slave who tries to kill Spartacus, in order to spare him from being crucified by the Romans. But that role was intended for an older, stronger man; someone more equal in size and stature, who would make a more convincing opponent in hand-to-hand combat. That *wasn't* Tony Curtis.

"Let me think about it and I'll get back to you." I hung up the phone. Tony seemed so down—I wanted to do something for him. I dialed Eddie at home.

"How's the writing coming?" It was now a running gag

between us. Every time Eddie Lewis told someone he was writing *Spartacus*, it embarrassed him. He wasn't an actor but he had to do a lot of acting.

We both knew it was necessary; the blacklist was still a real threat. The revelation of Dalton Trumbo's involvement with *Spartacus* could shut down the entire picture. So Eddie continued to play the producer-turned-writer, a charade he hated.

"Tony Curtis just called me. He wants to be in the picture."

"Jesus, maybe *he* could play Varinia!" Tony had just done drag with Jack Lemmon and Marilyn Monroe in the new Billy Wilder movie, *Some Like It Hot*.

"What do you think, Kirk? The accent would work perfectly. She'd be a slave girl from the Bronx." Eddie was still laughing.

"Hey, I'm serious. He wants in. It doesn't need to be a big part, just a couple of scenes. What can we find for him?"

Eddie was quiet for a moment. When he spoke, the laughter was gone from his voice. "I think it's a lousy idea, Kirk. But he's *your* friend. I'll call Dalton and get him working on something for Tony."

"Thanks." Eddie was right. I *was* letting Tony play on our friendship. But it was my decision and I'd made it.

"Okay, Kirk, I'll see you tomorrow at the office. Oh wait, there's one more thing."

"What is it?"

"Dalton keeps asking me about Nixon. What should I tell him?"

A few months earlier, I was surprised to get an invitation to a private event in Washington, D.C., with Vice President Richard Nixon. He was running for president to succeed Eisenhower, so I assumed he was trying to find some support in Hollywood. Maybe he thought my friendship with John Wayne would make me sympathetic to him. I wasn't really interested in politics, but I accepted the invitation anyway.

When Dalton Trumbo heard about it, he was tremendously excited. With the election just two years away, he thought Nixon would be looking for ways to moderate his image as a virulent anti-Communist. (Years later, after he became president, Nixon flew to Beijing and met with Mao Tse-tung. People said, "Only Nixon could go to China.")

Dalton figured Nixon might be receptive to a pitch from me about ending the blacklist. Signing it "Sam," Dalton wrote an eloquent letter, giving me ammunition for our possible meeting. It read, in part:

> Eleven years later, I doubt that there are five members of the Communist party in all of Hollywood. Most blacklistees have been out of the party for years. Some of them have become conservatives, some have become democrats, and some have maintained a generally socialist point of view. But to the last man they cannot in conscience admit the right of any legislative committee to judge their loyalty. Beyond this, they view a forced confession of former guilt or stupidity as no different in principle from the public confessions that have characterized Russian justice, or the brainwashing that is charged to the Chinese. For this reason, and this reason only, scores of them have kept silent and suffered the consequences. I do think there are very, very strong arguments against the blacklist . . . and I have taken the liberty of setting down a few notes, in a style which I hope is cool enough and detached enough that they might be left in the possession of Mr. N[ixon] without compromising the person [Kirk] who turned them over to him.

The event was subsequently postponed, but Dalton kept bringing Nixon up with me. He had watched then-Congressman Nixon sit silently during the House Un-American Activities Committee, while J. Parnell Thomas was banging his gavel and issuing contempt citations. Dalton believed that Nixon was never really comfortable with the witch hunts.

I was skeptical. Nixon would have the credibility to say it was time to end the blacklist, but would he have the guts?

Ending the call, I said to Eddie, "Let 'Sam' know that I'm still working on getting in to see Nixon."

I did make a trip to the East Coast before the end of the year, but it wasn't to see Nixon. It was a trip I didn't want to make. Ever.

The week before Thanksgiving, my mother called me. This was strange. My birthday wasn't until next month. She wanted to know when I was coming to see her next. That was even less like her. She never pressed me to come visit. Then it hit me.

When my plane landed in Albany, New York, a limousine was waiting to take me to the assisted-care home where my mother was living. It was her idea to move there. Initially, I'd been against it.

Later, I realized that it was difficult living with my sister Fritzi and her two kids. Whenever Fritzi went out, Ma ended up taking care of the kids. It had become too much for her.

I arrived at the home. A female supervisor was waiting for me.

"I'm so glad you came, Mr. Douglas. We're moving your mother to the hospital tomorrow."

She escorted me to Ma's room. I looked at the door; her name, "Bryna," was printed on it.

She opened it a crack and peered in. "She's asleep. Don't stay long." I went in, closing the door behind me.

I pulled up a chair and sat down beside her. Her arm hung loosely over the bed. I took her hand, held it gently, and listened to my mother's labored breathing. I looked around the room. There was the big television set I had given her. It made Ma very popular in the house. Everyone wanted to visit her and watch their TV shows. My eyes drifted to the dresser and I couldn't help but smile; there was a half-empty bottle of scotch. Ma never drank in her whole life, but a year ago, the doctor recommended she take a shot of whiskey every day to stimulate her heart. Ma got to like that remedy, and I'm sure she'd sneak a second shot in.

On the table, I saw two very familiar objects—two candlesticks that my mother had brought from Russia. They must be more than a hundred years old, made of pewter that was shined endlessly. Of course, tomorrow, Friday, was the Sabbath. My mother was ready to light the candles and say the prayer. I was awakened from these reveries by the weak voice of my mother.

"Issur?"

"Hello, Ma, it's me."

"My big-shot son."

"Oh, Ma, you always say that. But I like it."

"Az men ruft on dayn nomen, es tsitert di gantse erd."

"Ma, the whole world does *not* tremble when they say my name."

Whenever my mother got emotional, she always spoke Yiddish.

"They know your name too. Remember when we drove the limousine to Times Square?" When *The Vikings* opened, I took her to see the huge BRYNA PRESENTS sign covering the block.

"Yes, I remember. I remember," she said. The memory brought a small light to her tired eyes. She started coughing. There was a glass of water on the bedside table. I held it to her lips. She took a sip.

"Ma, I started a new picture."

"What picture?"

"*Spartacus*. A man called Spartacus."

"Sparti-kus. A good man?"

"Oh yes, Ma. Very good."

"Action?"

"Lots of action."

"Do you get hurt?"

"No, Ma, I don't get hurt. But at the end I do get crucified."

"Huh?" She looked confused.

I smiled, reassuringly. Taking her hand, I said, "It all ends happily."

Would she ever be able to see it? I was fighting back tears. I saw the kind face of the young girl who came from Belarus, married a cruel husband, and had seven children. Her last wish was to not be buried next to Pa. How she must have suffered.

Suddenly, her hand became limp. Her eyes closed. Had she stopped breathing?

I was terrified. "Ma! Ma!"

Her eyes opened, and she looked up at my terrified face. She took her hand from mine and extended her index finger. Where was she pointing? I turned around. I couldn't believe it. She was pointing at the whiskey bottle.

I looked down at my mother. Now *she* was smiling.

Director Anthony Mann rehearses the cast.

CHAPTER SIX

"If we punished every commander who made a fool of himself
. . . we wouldn't have anyone left above the rank of centurion."

—Laurence Olivier as Marcus Crassus

THE ALARM CLOCK WENT OFF at 6:00 a.m. Damn. I slammed it hard and thought of grabbing another hour of sleep. No way. There was too much to do. I looked over at Anne, burrowed under the covers. Now that we had two small children, sleep was precious to her. Fortunately, she slept through most of my now-daily predawn departures for the set.

It was Thursday, January 15, 1959. Since coming back from my mother's funeral, I'd hurled myself headlong into preproduction on *Spartacus*. In less than two weeks, shooting would start in Death Valley, California.

Larry Olivier was due on the lot that day for his costume

fitting as the regal General Crassus. I was being fitted for my various Spartacus outfits—the slave rags and the rebel leader's battle garb. We were scheduled to have lunch together after our camera tests.

This would also be Tony Mann's first meeting with Olivier. I knew he was nervous about directing the legendary Sir Laurence. Who wouldn't be? Ten years earlier Olivier won the Oscar for *Hamlet*, having directed himself in the part. Tony knew that Olivier originally wanted to direct this picture too. That certainly wouldn't help his confidence level in dealing with Larry, not to mention Laughton and Ustinov, who were themselves accomplished actor-directors.

I drove over the Cahuenga Pass to the Universal lot. The sun was just coming up over the vast San Fernando Valley hillside where the studio's many soundstages were scattered like giant aluminum and cement bunkers.

True to his word, Lew Wasserman had just purchased all that acreage for the impressive sum of $11.25 million. Milton Rackmil made the announcement, welcoming his new "partners" at MCA, but assuring the world that the studio itself would still be run by him. Lew stood off to the side of the press conference, saying nothing. He knew that Rackmil's days were already numbered, even if Milton did not.

Our small army of camera operators, electricians, set decorators, makeup artists, prop men, wardrobe women, grips, gaffers, and gofers was swarming over the lot that Lew bought. They already numbered well over a hundred people and that figure was growing steadily. And we hadn't shot a single frame of film.

When I got to my dressing room, I was drawn instantly into the vortex of frenzied activity that engulfed *Spartacus*. As both executive producer and star, the buck (and with this film, there would be a lot of them—the budget was now up to $5 million and still climbing) stopped with me.

Even in my makeup chair, a constant stream of people threw questions at me.

Alexander Golitzen, the art director, brought over a genuine Roman medallion he'd received from Naples and also showed me the replica that studio artists had made from it. Did it look accurate?

A messenger arrived with the latest version of the script, along with a note from "Sam Jackson." When could he expect to hear from me with my comments?

The phone on the left side of my chair rang. Ed Muhl, Universal's production chief, was on the line with his daily call about the rapidly escalating budget.

While I was talking to Muhl, the other phone rang. It was Technicolor, the company we were using for its new Technirama color process. It still had some bugs in it and the head of the company was on the line to apologize.

"Hang on, Ed," I said to Muhl. I grabbed the other phone. "Listen, we've announced that we're shooting *Spartacus* in Technirama. You don't want to make a liar out of me, do you?" I gave the phone back to the production assistant, and Muhl was still waiting patiently on the line.

"Jesus, Ed," I continued, right where I'd left off. "We've been through all this. *The Vikings* came in over budget too, and UA got it all back in spades. They're making money hand over fist on that picture. You've got to *trust* me on this. All right. Yes. Thanks, I will. Good-bye."

While this chaos was happening all around me, bronze makeup was being applied to my face, arms, and bare torso for the camera test that Kirk Douglas, actor, was scheduled to have at 10:00 a.m.

It was a typical day at the office.

I poured myself a cup of coffee from the large thermos that was always by my chair as Eddie Lewis came into the dressing room. He clicked his heels and gave me a Nazi salute. "Heil Spartacus."

"What's that mean?"

"I heard you were talking to Sabina in German."

"Not anymore. She's got to work harder on her English. But I like her."

As I sipped my coffee, Eddie filled up a mug of his own. "I didn't know you speak German."

"Yeah, French too, and a little Italian. What did you think I was *doing* when I made those pictures in Europe?"

He grinned. "I won't answer that."

"Don't you speak any languages?"

"Yeah, Yiddish." Eddie chuckled and sipped his coffee.

"Sit down, Eddie. I want to tell you something." Eddie looked at me curiously for a moment, but he complied. He grabbed a chair and pulled it over toward mine. I said to the young production assistant, "Can you give us a minute?" The boy left.

I turned back to Eddie. "Listen, I know how much of a schmuck you feel playing the fake writer."

"I hate it." He was emphatic.

"But I want you to know how much I appreciate it, and it won't be for much longer."

"Promise?"

"I promise." I stood up. "Let's go to the set."

I strode toward the set for my camera test. Eddie walked along with me. "Sabina's doing a photo shoot today for *Life* magazine," he said.

Our selection of this unknown German girl to star in a major American motion picture had already made Sabina Bethman a huge celebrity back in her own country. Now the Hollywood press corps was discovering her too.

"That will be great publicity for the picture," I said, as Eddie raced to keep up with me. "Are we good with the rest of the cast?"

"We've got John Gavin for Caesar. He's a good-looking kid;

I think you'll like him. And we nailed down Nina Foch, John Ireland, Joanna Barnes, John Hoyt, Herbert Lom, and your old buddy John Dall for those other open parts."

"What about Woody?" Woody Strode was a decathlon star at UCLA and one of the first players to break the color barrier in the NFL. Now an actor, he was my top choice to play Draba, the Ethiopian slave who is paired with Spartacus in a fight to the death.

"I think we've got him too," gasped Eddie, out of breath from our on-the-run casting meeting. We'd arrived at the set.

I just woke up from a nap and reread these last few pages. Setting them down on paper was tiring. Writing about myself almost fifty-three years ago is a strange experience. I'm learning a lot about the man I was back then; I'm not sure I like him very much. Burt Lancaster once introduced me at a dinner by saying, "Kirk would be the first person to tell you he's a difficult man to work with. I would be the second." I laughed. The truth didn't hurt.

I haven't been that guy in many years, the man Dalton Trumbo described as "running so fast in such tight circles that he collided with his own spoor."

At ninety-five, I don't have a need to prove anything to myself anymore. Time is so precious. It's the only thing you can't get back. Instead of rushing so fast through life, I move at a far more measured pace. Age and circumstance—a stroke, a helicopter crash, knee surgery, and a pacemaker—have all slowed me down. Even if I wanted to, I couldn't race around like I did when I was making Spartacus.

I won't lie and tell you that I like getting older. I don't. What I do like is what my age allows me to see. My stroke taught me a lot. I discovered the magic of silence. It talked to me. When I was first recovering, I sat in my room and listened with my eyes shut. When I opened them, I always saw Anne standing there—beautiful.

Now I take time every day to walk in my garden, admiring the

*roses—God's creation. When I was younger, busier, I never really
saw the subtle color of roses. How could I have missed that for so
many years?*

After lunch with Olivier, I finally made a painful phone call
that I'd been avoiding—I had to tell Gene Tierney she wouldn't
be playing Varinia. This was a particularly difficult call to make.

It was very hard to tell her she didn't get the part. And it
wasn't easy for her to hear—maybe because she was afraid this
meant her career might really be over.

Eddie Lewis walked in as I was saying good-bye to Gene. He
knew by the expression on my face that it hadn't been an easy call.

"How'd she take it?"

I just shook my head slowly.

Eddie roused me from my melancholy by swiftly changing
the subject.

"Hey, did you know that Tony Mann took Ustinov over to
Dalton's house to meet him?"

"Yeah, I heard that from Larry at lunch today. He was a
little peeved that Peter was let in on the secret of 'Sam Jackson'
before he was."

"He's right," Eddie said angrily. "Tony should have asked us
before he took Peter out to Dalton's house. That wasn't smart.
Ever since he got here Peter's been so far up Tony's ass he could
draw a map of his colon."

"Well, he did draw a *sketch* when was he was at Dalton's
house," I said, laughing. "He showed it to Olivier this morning.
Larry described it to me—it's a picture of Laughton with a dagger in his back. Peter told him, 'This is what I'm going to do to
Charles.' Larry thought it was hysterical."

"So Olivier and Laughton really don't get along at all?" asked
Eddie, concerned at the prospect of these two titanic talents
going to war with each other on the set of *Spartacus*.

I got up to leave. "Olivier thinks Laughton is jealous of him.

Larry actually *likes* Charles, but Charles is a perpetual victim. He thinks everyone is always out to make him look bad. And Peter is playing the diplomat between them."

"Yeah," said Eddie, darkly. "The diplomat with the dagger. What are your plans this weekend?"

I looked back at Eddie, grinning. "What the hell do you *think*? Now I have to take Larry over to meet Trumbo too. He doesn't want Peter to be the only one in the cast with a direct line to 'Sam Jackson.'"

On Sunday afternoon, I picked up Olivier. He was staying in Hollywood with Roger Furse, the British production and costume designer who, on Larry's recommendation, we'd hired for *Spartacus*. Roger and his wife, Inez, were providing Larry with the emotional support he needed. Larry and Vivien were heading toward their inevitable breakup. Larry's melancholy was palpable. If anything, he appeared even more distracted than he was when we were making *The Devil's Disciple* over the summer. And that had been a relatively brief shoot.

I smiled at him as he got into my car. Each of us was wearing sunglasses against the harsh glare of the Southern California sky. "Well, Larry, at least it's a helluva lot warmer here than London," I said.

"I got a letter from Joan in yesterday's post. She tells me it's been raining regularly there, although as yet there has been no snow."

Shortly before leaving England, Larry began a romance with a young British actress, Joan Plowright. Over lunch, Larry told me he'd been teaching himself to type so that he could write to her every day.

"How's the typing coming?" I asked, as I navigated onto the freeway.

"Splendidly," he replied, though his tone belied the word. "A, S, D, F, G . . ."

"L, K, J, H," I replied, finishing the typing lesson mantra

that I'd learned long ago back in Amsterdam. I looked over at Larry, grinning.

"If this acting thing doesn't work out for us, perhaps we can fall back on our secretarial skills." Larry smiled wanly as he said this. He was still tremendously distracted, thinking of home and the complicated life he'd left on hold.

I was beginning to worry about Larry's ability to focus on *Spartacus*—a six-month commitment that would keep him apart him from his new love, while still legally bound to Vivien. Consummate professional that he was, Larry successfully concealed his troubles from everybody at work. He tried to maintain a brave face with me too, but his eyes revealed a sadness that he probably preferred to hide.

I was really hoping that an enjoyable afternoon spent with "Sam Jackson" would provide Larry with a much-needed distraction from his personal problems. Dalton, true to Trumbo form, didn't disappoint.

"Come in, gentlemen! Come in!" As if he were the maître d' of the Brown Derby, our host ushered us in to his small, book-lined living room with a sweeping gesture.

As we sat down, Dalton began bustling around behind the bar. His glass of bourbon was already half empty. I glanced at my watch—2:00 p.m. This was going to be a very lively Sunday.

"What will you have to drink? Larry? Kirk?"

"Vodka on the rocks," I said.

"Sam, if that's bourbon you're drinking, I'll have a bit of that," said Larry.

"It is, and you will have more than a bit. By the way, my friends call me 'Dalton' or 'Trumbo.' Either will do better than 'Sam,'" he said, winking as he poured.

"Thank you *very* much, Dalton," grinned Larry, accepting a huge tumbler of bourbon.

"To *Spartacus*!" shouted Trumbo, raising his drink high into the omnipresent cloud of cigarette smoke that hovered above him. We clinked glasses loudly and settled in for a long after-noon of hazy good fellowship.

After much talk about our respective families, the conversa-tion turned to the elephant who *wasn't* in the room, Charles Laughton. He and his wife, Elsa Lanchester, were on a six-week holiday in Hawaii. Charles had stopped in briefly at the studio for his wardrobe fitting right before they departed.

"I like Charles," said Dalton, "though he prefers Shakespeare."

Larry and I roared.

Larry said, "We're both at Stratford this season. I'm doing *Coriolanus* and he's doing *Lear*. He's asked me to direct him."

"Really?" I was surprised.

"Yes," said Larry, a smile playing at the corners of his mouth. He sipped his drink. "I refused, largely because it would have meant taking the place of a friend who had already accepted the position. I think Charles was secretly hoping I would say no, so that he could take personal offense."

"Now *that* sounds like Laughton," said Trumbo, pouring him-self another drink. His third? I'd already lost count. "We discussed the script and it went rather poorly. His sighs and grunts and soft reproaches somewhat unhinge me at close quarters. I think I will try to keep a little real estate between us from now on."

Trumbo was as gifted a raconteur as he was a writer. I looked at Olivier, again red-faced with laughter at this spot-on descrip-tion of Laughton. A quick thought flashed through my head: *I hope Larry has this much fun for the run of the picture. He deserves it.*

Abruptly, Larry stopped laughing. Staring off into the mid-dle distance, he said softly, "It's queer. He's envious of me, but I'm not his equal."

Dalton and I exchanged glances.

"I'm nowhere near up to him intellectually. I never really feel on the same level as he." He was musing aloud now, more to himself than to us.

Larry fell silent for a moment, reflecting on the still-painful memory. Carefully, he roused himself to his feet. "Where's the loo?"

Dalton pointed down the hallway and Larry, somewhat unsteadily, ambled off.

I walked over to the bar and poured myself another drink. "I told him on the way over here that we were seriously thinking of opening the picture in the desert, not in flashback from Crassus' point of view. He took it rather well. I think he's pleased with how you've beefed up his part."

"*He* may be pleased," observed Dalton, drily, "but Charles and Peter will see it as a Kirk-Larry coup."

I heard Larry coming back down the hall. "That's next month's problem. Tony Mann can play goodwill ambassador once we start shooting. I'm retiring."

"You're retiring?" Larry asked quizzically.

"From sobriety," I said, raising my glass toward Larry, as Dalton handed him a fresh bourbon.

"Eddie Lewis certainly had me fooled about the authorship of your fine work," said Larry, accepting the drink.

"No worse than what your beloved Bard did to that poor bastard Bacon," replied Trumbo.

Olivier chuckled. "Touché," he said. "Odd that you should mention the Bard. Only just now I was thinking about Shakespeare with regard to this fellow Crassus. You've written him brilliantly, Dalton. I just wonder . . ."

Here we go, I thought.

"I just wonder," repeated Olivier, draining his glass, which Trumbo moved quickly to refill, "if you see him as a hero or a villain? Or, perhaps, both?"

I answered for Dalton. "He sees himself as a hero, Larry. Crassus passionately loves Rome and is fighting to protect her from what he believes is a threat to her very existence. In his eyes, that makes him heroic."

Larry considered this thoughtfully for a moment, and Dalton filled the silence by asking, "Who's hungry? Cleo has dinner on the grill." I looked again at my watch . . . six-thirty. My God, we had been talking for over *four* hours.

We headed toward the rear of the house. The unmistakable aroma of sizzling steaks wafted toward us as we approached the backyard. Larry was walking arm in arm with Dalton, his new brother in bourbon.

"Trumbo, indeed, I believe *you* are the Bard! I had been thinking of playing Crassus with just a touch of the flirting femininity of Richard III and, by God, that new homosexual scene of yours has inspired me! That's *exactly* how I shall play him!"

The scene Larry was talking about was a risky one. It involved his character attempting to seduce his "body slave," played by Tony Curtis. We were going to have a tough time getting it by the censors, but I liked it.

As we walked outside, I wondered what Dalton's wife, Cleo, would think of Larry's surprising declaration, but she didn't even look up from the grill. By now she was inured to the steady stream of outrageous comments that were her husband's stock-in-trade. Why should his friends be any different?

"How do you boys like your steaks?"

The remainder of the evening was a blur of good food and tales that grew taller with each passing drink. Finally, around nine-thirty, we poured ourselves back into the car. "Home, James!" Larry said grandly, now completely in his cups.

Ten days later, our *Spartacus* army was finally on the march. The troop movements were massive. Planes, cars, buses, and trucks filled with actors, technicians, equipment handlers, and extras were dispatched in continuous waves to our base camp in Death Valley.

At 7:15 a.m., on Monday, January 26, a black Lincoln town car pulled up in front of our new two-story, five-bedroom home at 707 North Canon Drive in Beverly Hills. My bags had been packed for days. Anne was awake, as was our three-year-old, Peter. Eric, the baby, was asleep in his crib. I leaned in and kissed him. Peter clutched my ankles. "Daddy, stay!"

I swept him up in my arms and hugged him. "Daddy has to go to work. I'll be back soon." Passing him to Anne, I kissed her on the cheek. "I'll call you tonight, honey."

"Good luck, darling." She was stoic. Anne understood this was only the first of many trips I'd be making for *Spartacus*. Neither of us would have guessed that before this film was finished, our now-seven-month-old baby would be talking in complete sentences.

I arrived at the Furnace Inn Ranch, our location headquarters, shortly before noon. As I was checking in, I ran into Peter Ustinov and Tony Mann in the lobby. They were chatting and laughing together as I approached. Eddie was right; they'd already gotten real friendly. Maybe too friendly.

Ustinov said, "I was just telling Tony about my encounter this morning with one of the local residents. She saw all the crew activity and came over to me with a quizzical expression on her face."

Peter, a superb mimic, immediately switched into a high-pitched woman's voice.

"Excuuuse me, Mr. Ustinov," he said in an uncanny imitation of a female American tourist, "are you here making a motion picture?"

"Yes, madam. Indeed we are." This was said in his urbane British accent.

"What is the name of this picture going to be?"

"*Spartacus*."

"*Spartacle*? That's a funny name for a major picture."

Tony Mann doubled over in laughter. He was completely enthralled by Ustinov. Over the next few weeks, I would discover how in thrall to him he was.

The first week went very well. We shot the opening scene in the mine where Spartacus stops working to help a fellow slave who's collapsed in the grueling heat. Treating him like a rabid dog, the Romans beat him savagely until he snaps—locking his jaw on a soldier's ankle and only letting go after he is beaten into unconsciousness.

The things I had to do to make a living.

Tony seemed to have everything well in hand; the rushes looked good. We had some disagreement over how animalistic Spartacus should be in resisting the Romans, but nothing that seemed out of the ordinary when starting a new picture. Universal wanted a director who could make this huge train run on time. It seemed they were right about Tony.

Things were running smoothly.

Then we moved to the gladiator school run by Peter Ustinov's character, Lentulus Batiatus—and the wheels came off the train.

Ustinov's influence on the set was as outsized as his performance—a performance he was now improvising (if not improving) in almost every take. The problem wasn't Peter. Every actor, myself included, instinctively tries to interpret a part to his best advantage. Sometimes that helps a picture. Sometimes it doesn't. It's the *director's* job to know when and how to rein in that instinct.

Peter told Eddie that he was "happy to help Tony into the saddle any time he was getting ready for a shot." Of course he was. Tony was letting him run wild. The rushes from the second week couldn't have been more different from the first. In the scene with the slave girls, Peter's character throws them violently into their cell, then grabs one by the throat for having rebuffed his advances. Little of this was in the script. Worse, it was broad and over the top.

It soon became clear that Tony Mann had no interest in taking the reins back from Peter. He seemed overwhelmed by the enormity of the entire picture.

We had a problem. By the beginning of the third week, Universal knew it too. They were getting regular reports about

Mann's loss of control. We were running behind schedule, and the budget had now crept north of $6 million.

By Thursday, February 12, my "best friend," Universal production chief Ed Muhl, was in a panic.

"Kirk, you have to do something. This guy isn't cutting it. We can't afford to let this picture get away from us."

"Us? Us?! You guys were the ones who thought Tony was right for this picture. I never thought he was the right guy, but I went along with it. And now *we* can't afford to let this picture get away from *us*?"

"Now, Kirk . . ." Muhl began.

"What do you want me to do, Ed?"

There was a momentary silence. "You have to fire him."

Now *I* was silent. I knew he was right, but I've never enjoyed firing people. I'm no Donald Trump; I get no pleasure from it. And I liked Tony. He was a genuinely decent guy who was in over his head. That wasn't a capital crime, but apparently I was expected to be his executioner.

"Kirk, are you still there?"

"Yeah, I'm here," I said tersely. "We may have to shut down for a week or two until I can find another director, but I'll do it."

There was relief in Muhl's voice. "Thanks, Kirk. I really . . ."

"But listen to me carefully, Ed. This time *I'm* picking the director. You got that? Whoever he is, he's going to be my choice. Agreed?"

More silence. Reluctantly, Muhl said, "Agreed."

That night, I got very little sleep. It was almost as if *I* was the condemned man waiting for the sun to come up. When it finally did, I took a long shower and tried to clear my head. After I toweled off, I threw on my robe and walked to the front door to grab the morning paper. On the porch next to it was an envelope containing that day's script pages and the call sheet, the list of times we were due on the set. I glanced at the sheet: "Eleventh Day of Shooting—Friday, February 13, 1959."

Friday the thirteenth! Poor Tony.

He took it better than I could have hoped. He actually seemed relieved. Tony didn't say it, but I had the feeling he'd been looking for a graceful way out on his own. I told him that I owed him a movie and we'd honor his $75,000 contract in full. We agreed that his departure would be by mutual consent over "creative differences." Standard Hollywood-speak for a no-fault divorce.

Now, where in the hell was I going to find another director?

Woody Strode as Draba moving in for the kill.
Why is Stanley Kubrick sitting between us?

CHAPTER SEVEN

*"You may not be an animal, Spartacus . . . but this sorry show
gives me very little hope that you'll ever be a man."*

—Charles McGraw as Marcellus

"ARE YOU IN, STANLEY?"

Marty Ritt glared at the big pile of cash in the pot. With a
$500 buy-in and seven players, there was $3,500 on the green
velvet poker table. After putting in his ante, Kubrick left the
room to take a phone call—a long call. Now he was holding up
the Friday night game.

"Stanley! Get your ass back here. I'm down three grand,"
said Ritt.

The men sitting around the poker table looked up as the
boyish director walked slowly back from the kitchen. He had a
strange expression on his normally impassive face.

"Who was it, Stan?" asked Jimmy Harris, Kubrick's producing partner.

"Kirk Douglas."

Ritt scowled. "What do you want with that sonofabitch? He cost me my last picture."

"He just fired Tony Mann," said Kubrick, ignoring Ritt's comment. "He wants me for *Spartacus*. Tomorrow."

"Jesus," said Jimmy Harris, folding his cards. The poker game came to an abrupt end. "Are you sure you want to work with him again?"

"Well, he's better than Marlon. At least *he* makes up his mind," replied Kubrick. After six months of trying to get a western called *One-Eyed Jacks* off the ground, the mercurial Brando let Kubrick go and decided to direct it himself. That meant Stanley was available to take over *Spartacus*.

"What did you tell him?" asked Harris.

"For a hundred and fifty grand? I said, 'Get me the script.' It's being messengered over to my house right now."

"That sonofabitch," said Ritt, putting away the poker chips. "First he costs me my picture and now I'm out another three grand. Good luck to you, Stanley. You'll need it."

Later, one of the other players in the game relayed that whole exchange to me. I laughed because I'd had virtually the same conversation with Eddie Lewis after I told him I offered the job to Stanley. He thought I was crazy to work with him again.

The truth was that I was handing this cocky kid from the Bronx control of a picture whose budget far exceeded the combined total of all the movies he'd done before. Was Eddie right? *Was* I nuts?

Still, there were two things I knew about Stanley. First, even though he was only thirty, he had the talent and self-confidence to step in and take over a picture of this size. Second, his self-confidence often bordered on arrogance, a quality that could be a help or a hindrance when dealing with highly respected, but sometimes hard-to-rein-in, actors such as Olivier, Laughton, and Ustinov.

I'd soon find out how Kubrick would handle himself. After a series of intense meetings to bring him up to speed (*"No, Stanley, we're not going to reshoot in Death Valley; Tony's scenes are fine. They stay in the picture"*), we realized that we had reached a major disagreement over Varinia—Sabina Bethman.

Stanley saw the rushes from her two days of work. "She can't act. She has no range—there's no emotion."

"Stanley, give the kid a chance. She's trying hard. I think she can do it."

Stanley looked at me, expressionless. It suddenly struck me as beyond bizarre that a man so devoid of empathy was judging the emotional range of anyone, let alone this young girl.

"I've got an idea," he said. "I'll prove it to you."

Curious, I looked at him. "How?"

"Get her over here. I'll tell her that she's been fired. It won't be true—not yet—but *she* won't know that. Let's see how she reacts. I'll bet you a week's salary that she shows no emotion at all."

I was dumbfounded. In a calculated way—so like him—Stanley wanted to demonstrate dramatically that he knew precisely what he was doing.

It was a callous thing to do, but I'd given Stanley the job. I had to trust his judgment, even if I hated his methods. Eddie just threw his hands up in the air as if to say, *"You* hired him."

On Wednesday morning, I took Stanley Kubrick over to the set to introduce him to the cast and crew. Virtually everybody except Sabina Bethman and John Gavin was older than their boyish new director. Everyone had heard that Tony Mann was out, but the news of Stanley's selection as his replacement had not yet been made official.

We were shooting the scene in which Crassus (Laurence Olivier), Helena (Nina Foch), Glabrus (John Dall), and Claudia

(Joanna Barnes) are all seated high above the arena, looking down at the slaves-turned-gladiators they had chosen for a fight to the death for their entertainment.

Although not in the scene, Sabina was in costume as Varinia in case she was needed later. I briefly introduced her to Stanley at the side of the set and then walked him directly into the center of the arena.

"Friends, Romans, Countrymen . . ." I began. There was a small smattering of laughter. All eyes were on Stanley.

"Meet your new director, Stanley Kubrick." Murmuring, then awkward applause. "He has my full confidence and support and I know he'll have yours. Stanley, would you like to say something?"

Stanley looked uncomfortable, but his voice was strong. "Thanks, Kirk. This is a great picture and I'm honored to be a part of it. Let's get back to work."

I introduced Stanley to our veteran director of photography, Russell Metty. Like Tony Mann, Metty was a Universal favorite. During his twenty-five-year career as a cameraman, he'd worked with most of the top directors—everyone from Howard Hawks to Orson Welles. Now fifty-three, Metty was old enough to be Stanley's father. His gruff manner, along with his crew cut and ruddy complexion, made him an unlikely subordinate to this pale, tousled kid. To him, Stanley looked more like a beatnik than a boss. It was a bad match from the beginning. It would only get worse.

That night, at my invitation, Sabina Bethman came to my house. When I opened the door to greet her, Eddie and Stanley were in the living room. As I gave her a hug, Eddie walked up behind us.

"Hi, Sabina," he said, putting on his jacket. He turned to me, "Kirk, I have to go. I promised my wife I'd be home an hour ago." I glared at him, but I understood. He wanted no part of what was about to happen.

"Good night, Mr. Lewis. See you tomorrow," said Sabina.

Eddie shot me a quick glance. "Good night, Sabina."

I closed the door behind Eddie and took Sabina into the living room. Stanley was sitting on the couch, waiting.

"Hello, Mr. Koobik," she said, smiling warmly at her new director. Stanley ignored the mangling of his name.

"Sit down, Sabina," he said, not rising to greet her.

She took a chair opposite him and I remained standing in the hallway. Stanley wasted no time with pleasantries.

He took a sip of his soft drink, cleared his throat, and said coldly, "Sabina, you are not right to play Varinia. I have to get someone else."

I studied Sabina's reaction. Nothing. She registered no surprise, no shock, no indignation. In that instant, I knew Stanley was right. I owed him an extra week's salary.

For a few seconds, Sabina stayed frozen in her chair. Then, without a word, she got up and went directly to the bathroom.

The door locked. Immediately, her wailing was audible to Stanley and me.

"Stanley, I hope you're happy." I pointed down the hall to the sobbing Sabina. "You finally got some real emotion out of her."

Stanley looked at me, his heavy-lidded eyes expressing no remorse. Without a word, he walked to the front door and left.

I hurried down the hall and called through the bathroom door, "Sabina!"

"Lass mich in Ruhe!" (*Leave me alone.*) She was sobbing uncontrollably.

"Es ist nicht deine Schuld!" (*It's not your fault.*) I tried to comfort her by also speaking in German.

"Go away!"

"Sabina, the director wanted a star. All the other principals are stars. He insisted a star should play Varinia."

Through the door, she cried, "All Germany papers print stories—show pictures—me in *Spartacus*." Her sobs had subsided, but the anguish in her voice was painful.

"Meine Familie! What do I say?"

"Tell them the truth—the director wanted a star."

Suddenly, the crying stopped. There was only silence.

"Sabina?! Sabina, are you all right?" I started pounding on the door.

I heard the lock click and the door opened a crack. Sabina looked up at me, her face flushed. Still sniffling, she asked quietly, "What star?"

I heard myself blurt out the first name I could think of. "Jean Simmons."

"Oh," she said, taken aback at the name of an international star. "She is beautiful."

"Not as beautiful as you, Sabina. But she *is* a star, and our new director insisted on her."

She came out of the bathroom and I put my arm around her shoulder. We walked toward the front door. "Come, my Schatz. There's no shame in losing out to a star. It happens to all of us. It happened to me. Someday someone will lose a part, and the director will say, 'I need a star! Get me Sabina Bethman!'"

"Das würde mir helfen." (*That would help me.*) She had stopped crying.

We were at the car. I held the door open for her and she got in. "Beverly Hills Hotel," I told the driver. Then I leaned in and kissed her on the cheek. Now she was smiling, at least temporarily. I watched the car pull away. I felt so sorry for her. People say the definition of an actor is one who loves rejection. If that's true, this was Sabina's first defining lesson.

"Oh, my God!" In a flash, I realized what I'd just done. I'd let Stanley fire our leading lady without knowing if Jean Simmons was still available. What if she'd taken another picture? I ran back into the house and pressed the button for my office. "Please get me Jean Simmons. She's in Nogales, Arizona."

I slumped down in the chair. It was a tense few minutes. While I was waiting for the call to go through, I found myself looking at a picture of my mother that I always kept on my desk. I studied her half-smiling face. It had only been two months. I missed her.

The phone rang. I picked it up.

"Is that you, Jean?"

"Kirk?"

"Do you still want to play Varinia?"

"Yes! Yes, of course I do!"

"Get your ass up here pronto. We have costume fittings tomorrow."

"Whee! I'll be there!"

I looked again at my mother's picture as I hung up the phone. Her enigmatic smile looked back at me. My Mona Lisa. What was that word she used so much—*beshert*? It means "destined to happen." Some things are meant to be; maybe this was one of them.

Beshert.

What a fool I was for not having hired Jean right from the start. I'd been hung up on accents, when acting ability was the only thing I should have cared about. Anne had been right.

Jean and I had only one disagreement during the whole picture.

In the bathing scene, where she was supposed to be in the nude, Jean modestly insisted on wearing panties and a bra. This forced her to stay almost completely underwater so that the camera wouldn't pick up any part of the bra. Kubrick didn't like the shot and asked me to speak with Jean. I remember our conversation in that little stream very well:

KIRK: "Jean, it doesn't look right. You have to take off your bra."

JEAN: "I will not!"

KIRK: "Please understand, Jean, your bosoms will be buoyant in the water, but they will only see glimpses of them

instead of flashes of your bra."
Jean started grinning.
KIRK: "What's so funny?"
JEAN: "I bet you've had a lot of experience getting girls to
take off their bras."

She had me there. I started to stammer. Jean was laughing. Standing there in the water, she took off her bra and threw it on the shore. She had beautiful breasts.

After the bathing scene, we played the night scene between Spartacus and Varinia, lying together under the stars. Even though it's not in the script, I've always believed this was the night that the son of Spartacus was conceived. I thought we should dramatize this scene but Jean was against it.

Friday the thirteenth was a particularly unlucky day during the filming of *Spartacus*. A month earlier, Anthony Mann lost his job on that inauspicious date. Now, on Friday, March 13, with Charles Laughton's first arrival on the set, the main cast was assembled for our initial table read—a gathering where all of the principals sit together and read their parts aloud. The problem, of course, was that some had studied earlier versions of the ever-changing script. Olivier was still lobbying for an opening narration from his character, Crassus—the original flashback approach that had attracted him to play the part. He began the table reading with that version. Later, in an interview for the Criterion Collection's edition of *Spartacus*, Peter Ustinov described that painful scene in hilarious detail:

> And I remember that first reading with enormous clarity . . . Charles Laughton was in a dressing gown with his hair in curlers. And Olivier was dressed normally with a sports jacket. Kirk Douglas was dressed as a slave, and covered in dirt and grime. He had already been leaping from things.

And John Gavin was dressed in the full regalia of an important Roman chief of the period.

We started the reading, and it was quite different [from what we'd been sent previously]. It started out with Olivier in this version. And he put on a pair of glasses, very relaxed, and started reading the script. And it was like a litany in church, I couldn't hear what he was saying.

This went on, getting more and more awkward as we began to realize the script was rather different to what we had been led to expect, until Laughton suddenly stopped dead, and said: "I don't understand this scene. I thought for a moment, a little while back, that I might eventually understand it. Now I'm afraid that I'm *completely* lost."

And one smelled trouble.

We abandoned the reading. We all went back to our places and that was largely why Laughton became extremely difficult and wouldn't do what he was given. And that's when I was . . . asked to write the scenes between him and myself, which I was glad to do.

Ustinov's willingness to rewrite his scenes with Laughton helped mollify Charles, but there were other issues: we were having increasing problems with the press about the true identity of our principal screenwriter.

Both Walter Winchell and the *Hollywood Reporter* had printed items suggesting that Dalton Trumbo was the real writer on *Spartacus*. Hedda Hopper and the American Legion were predictably up in arms at the prospect of Communist sympathizers creeping back into the movie business. More congressional investigations were apparently in the offing. After a dozen years, no studio wanted to be the first to hire a blacklisted writer. I was only an independent producer. I had no power to change the system.

Luckily, not all the action in *Spartacus* took place *off* camera.

I tried to forget all the production problems, by doing my other job—acting.

Whenever possible, I did all my own stunts. In *Spartacus*, that had many risks—climbing to the top of a fifteen-foot-high fence and jumping off; hand-to-hand fight scenes with the slave guards; realistic swordplay with the Roman soldiers.

Even the preparation for the battle sequences was dangerous. I trained on a device of rapidly spinning swords, padded and sheathed in leather for rehearsal. To prevent bruised shins or a sharp crack to the head, I quickly learned to jump high and duck low.

Woody Strode, God bless him, kicked me so hard in our fight-to-the-death scene, I thought he'd broken my ribs. Woody's character of Draba is executed by Laurence Olivier's Crassus. As an example of what happens to rebellious slaves, Draba's body is strung up by his feet in frightening display. In 1959, there were no stunt doubles for a six-foot, four-inch black athlete-turned-actor. So Woody himself was hung upside down, motionless, for take after take.

It was amazing to me that no one was killed in the making of the picture. Sometimes it came close.

In the slave uprising scene, I found myself in a battle with my fellow actor Charles McGraw. The script called for me to drown him in a cauldron of soup. As I wrestled with McGraw, he resisted being held facedown in the big bowl of liquid. As he got closer and closer to being submerged, he pushed away from me. I pushed harder, shoving him down into the iron bowl. I felt terrible when I accidentally broke his jaw. McGraw finished the scene, but we couldn't use it. The shot in the film had to be done by his stunt double.

Stanley decided that a realistic depiction of ancient battle would include dismemberment. He hired amputees, actors missing legs, arms, even parts of their faces. (The art department created prosthetic body parts that could be hacked off during the scene.) One of these actors was an actual one-armed man, Bill Raisch. I was required to hack off his prosthetic arm, leaving only a bloody stump. This was the only time I refused to do a stunt. How would you like to swing a sword with a sharp edge at someone, cutting off his fake limb without injuring his real flesh?

Despite my misgivings, Stanley finally talked me into doing it. We shot it twice with me graphically cutting off Bill's "arm." Stanley called for one more take. I said, "No!" I wasn't going to risk hurting Bill Raisch with a third swing. Stanley looked up from the camera quizzically. I said, "We've *got* it, Stanley." He looked at me for a long moment and then said, "That's a print."

Many serious health problems occurred even when we *weren't* shooting. The daily call sheet began to resemble the nurse's station list in an emergency ward.

A month into production, Jean Simmons required female surgery that kept her bedridden for almost six weeks. When we got the news, Eddie Lewis said to me caustically, "Do you want me to call Sabina? I hear *she's* still available."

Tony Curtis was seriously injured while we were playing tennis at my house. He'd just returned my backhand shot, when suddenly he crumpled to the ground, grabbing his leg in agony. As I helped him limp off the court, he said he was fine; it was just a charley horse. The next day, the doctor told him otherwise. He'd split his Achilles tendon, a severe and painful injury that required a cast for his lower leg. This made it impossible to film any of his scenes, since he was bare-legged in every shot. We had to work around him for five weeks. How stupid did I feel? It happened at my house and on my court.

Even *I* fell victim to the curse of *Spartacus*. For the first time in my career, I couldn't answer the bell. The flu hit me so hard that I was out for ten days, another expensive delay. "Exhaustion," said the doctor.

I switched doctors.

Peter Ustinov and Charles Laughton: one witty story too many?

CHAPTER EIGHT

*"Corpulence makes a man reasonable, pleasant, and phlegmatic.
Have you noticed the nastiest of tyrants are invariably thin?"*

—Charles Laughton as Sempronius Gracchus

SOMEHOW, THROUGH ALL OF THIS, production on *Spartacus* continued. But all these unanticipated delays only added to the mounting budget. By spring, we were dealing with a $7 million production that was growing more expensive every day. It felt like a cross-country taxi ride with the meter on.

Still, *Spartacus* wasn't always stressful. There were many enjoyable moments. Whenever I could find the time, I loved to sneak over and watch the scenes between Charles Laughton and Peter Ustinov. Jean Simmons did too. This was risky, because she could barely control her giggling. On more than one occasion, she almost spoiled the take.

These two pros trying to outdo each other was really something to watch. It was like a game of verbal tennis, in which either player was capable of the most extraordinary shot, just inside the line. For the most part, I think Ustinov got the best of it. Of course, that was probably because, at my behest (and to Dalton's continued chagrin), he had *written* most of their scenes.

Returning one afternoon from one of those verbal jousts, I entered my office and my secretary immediately said, "I have Lew Wasserman on the phone for you." I grabbed the phone.

"Lew?"

"No, this is Joe McCullough. I'm a freelance writer and I hope you can help me."

I was taken aback. "Why did you say you were Lew Wasserman?"

"I couldn't get through to you any other way. I thought this would get your attention."

I controlled my impulse to hang up. "What do you want?"

"I'm trying to get an interview with Sam Jackson, the writer of *Spartacus*."

Uh-oh. Here we go again. "So why did you call *me*?"

"Well, you *know* Sam Jackson, don't you?"

"Of course I do."

"Can you tell me how to get in touch with him?"

"Contact the publicity department."

"I've done that. They never call me back."

"Well, I can't help you. They're calling me for the next shot. You'll have to excuse me, I've got to go." I hung up.

I didn't like being put on the spot. I also knew it wouldn't be the last time.

That night, I left the studio early. Since we started shooting *Spartacus*, it was very rare for me to get home before the kids were already asleep. As I entered the house, I heard their squeals. Anne was giving them a bath together in the tub. I walked into the bathroom and gave them each a soapy kiss. Then I went into the bedroom, kicked off my shoes, and stretched out on the bed. I was bothered by that phone call. After almost a dozen years, the damned blacklist was still real. And whether I liked it or not, I still had to play the game. Didn't I?

My thoughts were interrupted when Anne came into the bedroom.

"Hello, darling." She gave me another kiss, this time without soap bubbles. "Was today hard?"

"No, today was an easy one."

"Why do you seem so distracted?" It was uncanny how she could read me.

I only had to say one word. "Trumbo."

"Why is it so complicated? Why don't you just tell them he's writing the picture? He's doing a good job, isn't he?"

"You don't understand!" I heard myself shouting.

I was up off the bed, pacing the room. Anne watched me silently. She'd seen this movie before, many times.

"Of course the blacklist is wrong. I've spent months thinking of some way to break it. You can use a false name or a front and that's okay. But if you use the writer's real name, you're in trouble. It's crazy, but it's not the issue. If I rock the boat, we might lose everything—the picture, the company, my career, *everything*. We can't take that risk."

Sitting on the edge of the bed, Anne asked quietly, "Doesn't everybody already *know* he's writing it?"

"Universal doesn't." I was no longer shouting. "Those leaks in Winchell's column and in the trades had Ed Muhl all worked up. It took me half an hour to convince him that it was all just gossip, but they warned me that if Trumbo *was* involved in any way, they'd have a big problem releasing *Spartacus*."

Anne smiled. "I tell you, I really love your crazy country." She looked at me for a moment and then said, "Listen, Kirk, you're no dummy. You'll figure out how to handle it."

The blacklist. I even hated the name "blacklist." But, for once, maybe Anne was wrong. I had absolutely *no* idea how to handle it.

I also didn't have too much time to think about it. The quick change in directors and leading ladies had created an atmosphere of chaos on the set that was becoming more evident by the day. Dialogue was written, rewritten, discarded, rewritten again, then improvised.

Egos clashed like swords. Stanley Kubrick vs. Dalton Trumbo. Charles Laughton vs. Laurence Olivier. Kubrick vs. his cinematographer, Russell Metty. Peter Ustinov likened the on-set politics to a "Balkan government in the good old days."

One of the most memorable illustrations of these tensions involved Charles Laughton. Laughton, sensitive as he was brilliant, believed that his part was slowly being diminished. He chose to blame me for this.

I was in my dressing room, reading my script, when I heard a loud rap on the door.

"Come in!"

The door opened and in walked Charles, still clad in the senatorial Roman toga of his character, Gracchus. Even that bulky garment failed to conceal his ballooning weight. He had recently described himself as "looking like an unmade bed."

Laughton was carrying a small metal thermos. I knew it contained his favorite beverage, the "bull shot"—a toxic mixture of beef bouillon and vodka. His expressive face was contorted unmistakably in rage.

"Hello, Charles," I said cautiously. I started to reach for a glass, so he could pour himself a drink.

"I am not here on a social call, Mr. Douglas," he intoned imperiously.

"What's the matter?"

"I wish to inform you that I have notified my solicitors. I intend to take legal action against you and your company."

I stared at him, incredulously. This was the man I had written a fan letter to when I was a kid. Now he was going to sue me.

"Charles . . ." I began.

"Believe me, sir. I will cause you much trouble." He turned around to leave. Standing in the open doorway, blocking his exit, was the buxom blond actress Mamie van Doren. She was shooting another picture on the lot and had been assigned the dressing room next to mine.

"Excuse me, madam," he said haughtily. I watched as Charles tried to squeeze his enormous girth past Mamie's 35-23-35 figure. The image struck me as so ridiculous that I started chuckling.

Charles shot me a hostile glance over his shoulder. This only made me laugh harder. "Go ahead, sue me," I said to his back. "What the fuck do I care!"

As Charles retreated angrily, Tony Curtis appeared in the doorway, wearing only a small loincloth. Mamie's eyes lit up. "Tony, you're late." She'd been ogling him for weeks—not too subtly.

Tony winked at her. Mamie took the cue and went back to her dressing room with a smile too big for her face.

Then Tony asked me, "What was *that* all about with Laughton?"

"Who the hell knows? Charles thinks I'm cutting him out of the picture. It's just more of the same—everyone's got a beef."

"Yeah, you and Stanley were sure going at it earlier," said Tony. "I couldn't believe it. A month ago, you two were practically finishing each other's sentences—I thought I'd need to get you guys a room."

I glowered at Tony. This wasn't funny. Kubrick and I *had* been arguing a lot lately. The budget was still creeping up. We were now about to hit $8 million, and there was no end in sight. Stanley's exasperating genius was his blessing and our curse. He focused on every detail of every shot, causing frequent delays in the production. He'd completely taken over Russ Metty's job, consigning the veteran cameraman to the role of highly paid observer. Metty took it badly, mocking Stanley at every opportunity. Characteristically, Stanley wasn't bothered by the criticism—he simply ignored it and did what he wanted.

"You think this is easy?!" I shouted at Tony. "Why don't *you* try being the boss for a day?"

I wasn't angry at him. The Laughton episode had gotten under my skin. Charles relished being difficult because it made him the center of attention. I'd given him exactly what he wanted.

"Hail, Spartacus!" said Tony, playfully giving me a one-finger salute as he headed toward Mamie's dressing room.

"To hell with Spartacus!" I said, storming off toward the set.

My battles with Stanley finally reached their breaking point that same day. The issue was the pivotal scene in which the captured Spartacus and his remaining troops are all in chains, awaiting their fate. I'd sent Stanley a note with what I thought was a pretty good idea for dramatizing the slave army's loyalty to their leader:

> The battle is over and in a gully near the battlefield, all the prisoners are being rounded up; a large group of them are already chained and are sitting around, waiting for the next move. They are dejected; there is a hustle and bustle of Roman soldiers, Generals on horseback, mule wagons loaded down with chains for the prisoners . . .
>
> At a distance, on a rise, sits the noble Crassus on his white horse. He is surveying the assembly of prisoners . . . next to him is one of his Generals. At a signal from Crassus, his subordinate General rides down with a group of slaves.
>
> In a loud voice, he announces to them that whoever identifies the living or dead body of Spartacus will be set

free. There is a sudden, silent hush over all the prisoners. Spartacus gets up . . .

Suddenly, Antoninus jumps up with his arm waving, "I am Spartacus!" David the Jew follows suit. In short order, the hundreds and hundreds of slaves are all jumping up, yelling in a happy vein, "I am Spartacus!"

Crassus stands alone, surveying this mockery of his victory by a group of doomed men. He whirls away on his horse, in his ears the crescendo of exultant slaves all yelling in unison . . . "Spartacus . . . Spartacus . . . Spartacus!"

Kubrick didn't reply to my idea, which only added to my irritable mood.

We were shooting a scene where I was on horseback. As I mounted my beautiful brown mare with the white stripe down her face, I saw Stanley setting up for the shot. He was dressed in the same blazer and khaki pants that he'd worn every day since I first introduced him as the new director. I'd heard grumblings from the crew that Stanley's lack of concern about his apparel was a sign that he didn't care what they thought of him. This was true; he *didn't* care. But a more experienced director would have understood that it was always better to have the crew with you than against you.

I trotted over to Stanley. "Hey, Eisenstein," I called down to him. I knew Stanley admired the Russian director. He looked up at me from behind the camera.

"Have you ever thought about changing your clothes?" I said.

He looked at me blankly, as though I'd asked him if he was a Martian.

"No," he muttered distractedly, looking back through the viewfinder of his camera.

"Goddamn it, Stanley, I'm talking to you!"

He looked up at me again, still expressionless.

"Stanley," I said calmly. "It would help if you'd bother to

change your clothes every now and again. People would think you cared enough to make a good impression."

"I don't," said Stanley, simply. He started to look through the camera again. I rode my horse right up to him.

"Stanley." My voice was low, but now angry. "*I* care."

Out of the corner of my eye, I could see all the crew members watching us carefully. Stanley looked up from his viewfinder but said nothing.

"Go to the store tomorrow and buy yourself some new clothes. I'll pay for them."

"I don't . . ." he began.

"Stanley, this is not a discussion. You're going to wear new clothes to the set tomorrow. Understand me?"

Kubrick began to redden, but there was still no response. I rode my horse so close to him he had to back away from the camera.

"I asked you a question," I said.

"Yes," he replied finally, although his tone indicated he meant no.

I inched my horse even closer to Kubrick. He was now backing up with every advance. Some of the dust kicked up by the horse was getting into his eyes. He brushed his face and looked at me angrily.

"And while we're on the subject of understanding, there's something else I want *you* to understand. When I send you a memo about shooting a scene, I at least expect an answer. I sent you that note about the 'I am Spartacus' scene and you haven't even bothered to respond."

"That's because I don't want to do it," said Kubrick, coolly. "It's a stupid idea."

That was the wrong thing to say.

I pushed the horse right up against him. She nosed him back against the wall, pinning him there.

"Listen, you little prick," I said. "I've gone along with you on everything and you've been right about most of it. You were right about cutting out almost all of my dialogue at the beginning of the movie. You were right about the scene between Varinia and Spartacus just touching hands—it's much better the way you shot it. You've been right about making the battle scenes more realistic. It's cost us a helluva lot of time and money, but I've supported you every step of the way."

"Kirk . . ." he began.

"Shut up. This *may* be a stupid idea but we're going to try it. If it doesn't work, we'll cut it out, but we're going to shoot it." My voice was now loud enough for the whole crew to hear. They were hanging on every word.

For the first time, Stanley looked a little intimidated. I hadn't wanted to do this in front of the entire crew, but perhaps it was a good thing. He was enormously talented—to a fault. With a little humility, I really believed he could be a great director.

Stanley, literally with his back to the wall, capitulated. "I'll set it up. We'll shoot it tomorrow."

I looked down at him and smiled. "Thanks, Stanley," I said. "And get yourself something other than a blazer, okay?"

With that, I turned my horse around and galloped off the set. Maybe I was imagining it, but I thought I heard a smattering of applause as I rode away. Or maybe I'd seen too many Tom Mix movies as a kid.

We had now been in production for four months. Larry was about to return to England for his highly anticipated run as Coriolanus at Stratford-on-Avon. I was going to miss working with him. Besides being a brilliant actor, he was always gracious to everyone, cast and crew alike. A true gentleman.

That weekend, Anne and I drove down to our house in Palm Springs, so I could rest and get away—at least briefly—from the trials of *Spartacus*.

On Sunday, after sleeping for almost twenty-four consecutive hours, I was awakened by a call from Jean Simmons. Finally, some good news. Her doctor had cleared her to come back to work, after an absence of almost six weeks. I breathed a sigh of relief. We could finally stop shooting around her.

After my welcome call from Jean, I put on my swim trunks and went out to rest by the pool. After about an hour, the sun began to set, casting lengthening shadows over the desert. The nearby mountains darkened into silhouettes as they slowly disappeared from view.

I had just dozed off again when I heard Anne's voice calling to me, "Pick up the phone—Eddie Lewis."

Dazed from sun and sleep, I reached for the extension phone on the poolside table. "What's up?"

"I just got a telegram from Trumbo."

"A telegram?"

"Yeah, it's addressed to both of us."

"Read it."

I heard the sound of an envelope being torn open.

"'The two actors,'" began Eddie, "'neither of whom is a writer, have met and arrived at mutual decisions about how a writer should write.'"

I interrupted. "*Which* two actors?"

"He obviously means Laughton and Ustinov. Let me read you the rest: 'I recognize no such authority, nor any precedent for people to become creative in fields in which they are, so far as my knowledge follows them, unqualified. I have rewritten as much as I intend to. Let the real creative people take over and improve my feeble efforts, and let them also take a credit which it has been mutually assumed shall be assigned to no one.'"

"Is he saying he won't rewrite any more of the Laughton-Ustinov scenes? What does he . . . ?"

"Kirk, hang on a second, there's someone at the door."

After a moment Eddie came back on the line. "Well, we just got another telegram."

"From Sam Jackson?"

"Yes—are you sitting down?"

"Go ahead."

He began reading again: "'Twenty minutes after my wire regarding the two actors, I have arrived at the decision that I quit this picture absolutely.'"

"Shit," I said.

"Wait, there's more," said Eddie. "'Inadvertent, continued insults do not disturb me. Calculated ones, in which what I have always felt was an honorable profession, are too degrading for me to endure. There are more talented men in the art of acquiescence who will serve you better throughout your careers.'"

I exhaled audibly. No one wrote outrage better than Dalton, even in a telegram.

Eddie finished delivering the bad news. "Then he signs it, 'With a good deal of affection, but with far more resentment and disgust. Sam.'"

"Jesus, Eddie. This is a disaster."

"Yeah. We're already two months behind schedule."

"This could shut us down permanently."

There was a long pause.

"Kirk? Are you still there?"

"No, I'm not. I need to deal with this right now. Talk to you later."

I hung up quickly, threw on clothes, and jumped in my car.

As I headed toward the freeway for the two-hour drive up to Trumbo's house, I tried to sort out what I was going to say to him.

He was right, of course. The continued rewriting of his script pages—often on the fly—*was* degrading. Dalton Trumbo was a man of considerable pride. It was going to be a very difficult conversation, and he might still quit the picture.

I pulled up to his house. His battered old car was parked in the driveway. Good, he was home. I rang the doorbell. From inside the house, I heard the parrot repeatedly squawking a phrase. It sounded like, "On the rocks! On the rocks! On the rocks!"

The door opened and Dalton appraised me coldly. "I wondered how long it would take you to get here."

I grinned. "I got a telegram from your 'friend' Sam Jackson. Is he here?"

"No, I killed him. We just buried him in the backyard. It was a lovely ceremony. Too bad you missed it." He turned around and walked back toward his study without even a handshake.

I followed him and tried to lighten the mood. "Why didn't you call me? I would have sent flowers."

"It doesn't matter; he won't be missed."

Now he was behind the bar, pouring drinks. "Certainly not by anyone who's read his work," he added.

Taking a deep swallow of my drink, I asked Dalton pointedly, "What will it take to bring him back to life?"

"It's too late. Easter was last month. Besides, you're a Jew. You don't believe in resurrection."

I put my drink down on the bar and moved closer to him. "We can't finish this picture if you quit now."

He stared at me intently. "I've written a quarter of a million words on this picture and I have no idea if a single one of them is going to wind up on the screen. I won't work that way anymore."

"Dalton, you're right. I'm sorry. If we hadn't been so rushed from the beginning, I would have done it better. That's my responsibility. You blame Stanley or Peter and Charles but the buck stops with me."

Despite himself, Trumbo smiled slightly. "Oh, so now you're Harry Truman."

"Yes," I said, relieved to change the subject. "At least Truman finally came out against the blacklist." In the past few months, the former president had made several strong public statements calling for an end to the Hollywood blacklist.

"It took him long enough," replied Dalton, acidly.

Trumbo served almost a year in jail for saying essentially the same thing that Harry Truman was now being *praised* for saying.

Back then, a supportive statement from the White House would have made a big difference. But as president, when it mattered, Truman stayed silent. Worse, he ordered all federal employees to take loyalty oaths.

I realized at that moment what I needed to do. It was right there in front of me all along—why hadn't I seen it?

I took a deep breath. "I *don't* want Sam Jackson back. Let's leave him dead and buried. I want Dalton Trumbo."

He studied me hard. I knew this was the only solution, but would Dalton believe me?

"Let me understand this," he said skeptically. "You're saying if I come back to work, you'll tell Universal that *I'm* the writer on *Spartacus*?"

I paused. This was tricky. "No . . ." I began.

Dalton started shaking his head in disgust.

"Hold on, hold on. Hear me out. *No*, I'm not going to tell them you're writing this picture. That could blow everything up. But when it's in the can, not only am I going to tell them that you've written it, but we're putting your name on it. Not Sam Jackson's name, *your* name—Dalton Trumbo—as the sole writer."

I could feel my heart pounding. Even as I was saying the words, I was still trying to convince myself that this was worth the risk.

He stared at me, not speaking. I sensed his resolve was weakening.

"Dalton, stick with me and let's get this picture finished. I give you my word that's what will happen."

He looked at me thoughtfully. "Where's Eddie?" he finally said.

"Dalton, you *know* Eddie. He's completely on your side. But we're not going to tell *anyone* until we're finished, or else it could kill the picture."

"So I just have to take your word for it? No witnesses, no paper, only your word?"

"Yes."

The parrot squawked, "On the rocks! On the rocks!"

We both laughed. The tension was broken.

I extended my hand. "Deal?"

Dalton Trumbo, never at a loss for words, needed only one.

"Deal," he replied. He held my grip for a long moment. His eyes, huge behind those glasses, were glistening.

We walked to the door. "Dalton, believe it or not, I want you to know that I was thinking about how I could put your name on the picture *before* I got those fucking telegrams from your dead friend," I said.

He looked startled for a moment, and then he burst out laughing.

I got in my car and drove home.

That night, I *did* tell Anne what I'd done. I tell her everything.

"I should have talked to you before I did this," I said apologetically.

She cut right to the heart of the matter, as she always does. "Do you think you did the right thing?"

I didn't answer her. I was looking down at the table, absentmindedly doodling while we were talking. I'd sketched a caricature of my own face. Big teeth, huge chin. The actor's obsession.

"Kirk!"

I looked up at her. "What?"

"Do *you* think you did the right thing?"

I hesitated. "Yes."

"Honey, you have to do what you have to do. It will all work out." Eric started to cry in his crib. She kissed me on the cheek and left the room.

"I hope you're right," I muttered, filling in the dimple in my chin.

The following day Sam Jackson was alive and well and submitting new pages.

Eddie was mystified. "What did you *say* to him?"

"I promised him five percent of the picture."

Eddie whistled. "And he took it?"

"He's *writing*, isn't he?"

I don't think Eddie quite believed me, but he didn't question it any further. Instead he said, "We just got a new batch of pages messengered over. Oh, and this came with it for you." Eddie handed me a wrapped package marked "KD." It felt like a book.

I took it into my dressing room and closed the door. I tore off the brown paper. It *was* a book—Dalton's antiwar novel, *Johnny Got His Gun*. He'd written it before he was blacklisted, and it had been out of print for years. I opened it to the inscription:

Dear Kirk,

    Here, for what it is, and for what I hope I still am, is the only existing copy of this book that is signed with the name to which I was born, and that other name you enabled me to acquire under circumstances that blessedly permit me to respect and to cherish both the new name and the new friend who made it possible.

Affectionately,
Dalton Trumbo
Sam Jackson

Dalton Trumbo/Sam Jackson–inscribed copy of Johnny Got His Gun

CHAPTER NINE

"Surely you know you're going to lose, don't you?"

—Herbert Lom as Tigranes Levantus

THE LIGHTS CAME UP IN the screening room. Nobody spoke. I looked around on either side of me. On my left, Eddie Lewis seemed shell-shocked. On my right, Dalton Trumbo, wearing an unseasonal overcoat and a floppy hat pulled low over his head, was slumped down in his folding chair. Under the cover of night, I'd snuck him on the lot in the backseat of my car, covered by a blanket, to see Stanley's first rough cut of *Spartacus*. No one at Universal knew Dalton was there.

I couldn't read his expression, but his body language said it all—he wished he had stayed home.

Kubrick was pacing back and forth at the front of the small

theater. The editor, Irving Lerner, and his assistant, Bob Lawrence, were huddled together just in front of me, furiously making notes.

I turned around. In the very back row, sitting alone, was Lew Wasserman. His normally impassive face was positively inscrutable. So far, Universal had spent more than $9 million on this film. Lew had personally guaranteed his studio "partners" that *Spartacus* would be a hit. After tonight's screening, that didn't seem very likely. Not likely at all.

Eddie was the first to speak. "The music will help," he said hopefully. We were all eagerly anticipating Alex North's score. A six-time Oscar nominee, North was in great demand, and landing him for *Spartacus* had been a real coup.

Stanley planted himself in a seat in the front row and started bouncing a tennis ball off the side of the screening room wall.

"We need more money," he said.

I looked at him like he was nuts. "We're two and a half times over budget and this is a mess! Why would the studio give us another dime?"

Stanley kept tossing the ball against the wall. He was talking to himself. "We need to shoot the final battle sequence. Right now all we've got is the aftermath. That's cheating the audience."

I turned around and looked up at Lew in the back of the screening room. He was putting on his hat. I started to walk up the aisle to talk with him, but Dalton grabbed my arm. "Let's get out of here," he said. When I looked back up the aisle, Lew was gone.

Irving Lerner approached me tentatively. "Don't worry, Kirk. We'll have another cut to show you within the week."

"No, you'll have it tomorrow," I said sharply. "I don't care if you have to work all night. Put cots in the cutting room. Just get me something I can show Universal."

"Please, Kirk. We need more time. How about four days? Today is Thursday, we'll have something for you by Monday night. We'll work tomorrow and all weekend."

Trumbo was tugging at my arm to leave. Stanley was still tossing the ball back and forth against the wall.

I shouted at Kubrick, "Good night, Eisenstein. I'll see you back here on Monday. And you'd better have something else to show me or I'm shipping you back to Brando."

Stanley ignored me. I heard him mumble something about "Spain."

Dalton, Eddie, and I walked out into the warm night air. Dalton kept his head down and made a beeline for my car. The parking lot was empty—we'd deliberately scheduled the screening for 8:30 p.m. and it was almost midnight.

I lingered for a moment with Eddie Lewis. "How bad is it?"

Eddie puffed on his pipe. "There's some tremendous footage, Kirk. You're great. Larry's great. Jean is wonderful. Peter is hysterical. Even that cantankerous old goat, Laughton, is fantastic. In fact, there's not *enough* of him. He was right about that."

"I *know* all that. The performances aren't the problem. The *problem* is there's no story. We tried the flashback angle to explain Spartacus' threat to the Roman Empire, but now it just feels like a ragtag bunch of convicts on a three-hour prison break."

"What does Sam think," Eddie asked, pointing at Trumbo, whose cigarette holder was sticking out of the passenger window of my car. There was no danger of him being spotted. He was enveloped in a cloud of smoke.

"I don't know yet," I said, starting toward the car. "I'm about to find out."

When I got behind the wheel, I said, "So, do you still want your name on this goddamn picture?"

Trumbo looked at me curiously. "More than ever."

Surprised, I glanced over at him. "Did you *like* it?"

"I need to see it again. Can you have someone run it for me—alone—tomorrow night?"

"Dalton, that's risky. We're taking a big chance just bringing you on the lot."

"I have to see it again."

I was silent for a moment. "Okay, I'll send a car for you tomorrow night. Wear a bigger hat."

He smiled slightly, lost in thought. After that, he said nothing the entire way home.

Dalton called me on Saturday morning. He fended off my questions about what he thought about the film after seeing it a second time. "I've been writing down some ideas. Let me put them all together on paper. You'll have them by Monday."

Later that day, I heard from Stanley. He said there would be another rough cut ready by Monday night. The only thing he told me was that the film would now open with me as a captive slave in the Libyan desert. No more flashbacks.

On Monday morning, a messenger boy arrived at my house as Anne and I were having breakfast with Peter and Eric. This was odd. There were no more script pages. What was being delivered at this hour?

I signed for the hefty envelope and saw "S. Jackson" scrawled in the upper left corner.

I tore it open as I walked back to the breakfast table. Inside were two typewritten documents—Dalton's carefully annotated analysis of the *Spartacus* rough cut. Every scene was broken down, even to the point of critiquing specific lines of dialogue.

He had written most of it over one weekend, and he couldn't have started until well after midnight on Thursday. My God, when did that man ever sleep?

Fascinated, I began reading. It opened with a quote from Churchill:

Never give in! Never give in! Never, never, never. Never—

in anything great or small, large or petty—never give in except to convictions of honor and good sense.

The Trummbbow clarion call! Encouraged by his fighting spirit, I continued to read:

> Let me make myself perfectly plain at the outset: more than any film I've ever worked on, I want this to be a great picture.
>
> I think it can be.
>
> From the opening of the film through the poem and the first real love scene between Spartacus and Varinia, sequence after sequence explodes onto the screen. The Roman scenes are, as we expected them to be, brilliant. But the delight and the surprise come in Kirk's character-ization of Spartacus. There is here a warmth, a tenderness, a strength that is nothing short of wonderful. I have never seen anything like that first scene in the cell between him and Varinia. Throughout the whole Capua sequence, the expression on his face whenever he looks at Varinia—a combination of reverence and wonder and yearning—con-veys the essential feeling of poetry.
>
> It is a very great achievement for both star and director; a piece of pure film for which no writer would dare take credit, since what has happened could never have been accomplished by words.

Then, as quickly as he'd inflated it, Dalton punctured my swell-ing pride when he put a numerical value on each of the main performances:

> In my scale we got 100% of what Olivier had to offer, a skimpy 90% of Ustinov's potential, no more than 65% of Laughton's, and approximately half of Kirk's and Simmons' . . .

I felt like I was on a dizzying roller-coaster ride. First, I was "warm, tender, strong, and wonderful," then he said I only gave half a performance. Talk about being damned with faint praise. I sipped some more coffee and kept reading:

> The first hour of Kirk is so lovely that with a few loops and re-cuts, plus contemplated re-writes, it is quite possible even now to get 90–100% of what he has to offer. He will automatically pull Simmons up with him. The possible result? We should have a lovely smash on our hands. And something more than a smash—a successful film financially in which we, as artists, shall all be able to take a quiet, personal pride.

Dalton then launched into his main argument: that there were two fundamentally conflicting views of the character of Spartacus and, as a result, of the film itself. Diplomatically (for him), he put it this way:

> I am going to try to point out as objectively as I can what I consider to be our past mistakes which have brought us to this present condition, not to arouse old differences between us, but to resolve them in a way that we shall not have to fear their repetition in the future. From the very beginning there have been two perfectly honest points of view on the nature of the Spartacus story. They are, I hope, objectively summarized below:
>
> LARGE SPARTACUS: The revolt of the slaves was a major rebellion that shook the Republic.
> SMALL SPARTACUS: That it was, in reality, more on the scale of a jail-break and subsequent dash for freedom.
>
> LARGE SPARTACUS: That it lasted a full year.

SMALL SPARTACUS: That it was much briefer duration.

LARGE SPARTACUS: That it involved a series of brilliant slave military campaigns, and the defeat of the best Rome had to offer.
SMALL SPARTACUS: That it was a simple dash to the sea.

LARGE SPARTACUS: That it was finally put down only by the overwhelming weight of three Roman armies against the single slave army.
SMALL SPARTACUS: That it was put down by one Roman army.

For seventy-eight pages, Dalton argued eloquently, sometimes caustically, and always persuasively, for his vision of the "Large Spartacus."

I had never read anything like it. As I turned each page, mesmerized, I thought, *They could teach this. It should be required reading for every would-be screenwriter, actor, or director.*

Trumbo/Jackson ended his manifesto with a passionate exhortation to return to battle. In his final section, self-deprecatingly titled, "THANK GOD HE'S THROUGH DEPARTMENT," he recalls why we began this film in the first place:

Our whole danger and our whole promise lies in the fact that we have aimed very high. If we for one moment forsake this high aim for a lesser one, we shall fall much lower than if we'd aimed lower in the first place.

Actually, this is not a matter of saving the picture: it's a matter of making it great. By the grace of God, and luck, a thousand mishaps to the schedule, the only part we could have cured is the part that is now physically possible for us to cure. Who could ask for more?

I say we can do it. Now goddam it, team, go, go, go!

Sam

It took eight more days before we reassembled under cover of darkness on the Universal lot—the same group: me, Eddie Lewis, the heavily disguised Dalton Trumbo (he had changed hats), Stanley Kubrick, and his editing team of Irving Lerner and Robert Lawrence.

The only one missing from the prior screening was Lew Wasserman. I had promised him that I'd call him immediately after I watched it.

The lights went down and the screen filled with designer Saul Bass' magnificent opening titles.

Anthony Mann's beautifully shot opening sequence in the desert now began the film. Olivier's flashback narration was gone.

Despite Stanley's reluctance to use anything he hadn't shot, even he had to acknowledge that Mann's footage was excellent. The Death Valley setting translated onto the screen exactly as we had hoped—bleak, desolate terrain where slaves lived short lives of hard labor and hopelessness.

Peter Ustinov's character, Batiatus, appeared on the screen. I watched in amusement at the completely improvised business where he inspects Spartacus' mouth before buying him. I thought it was a great idea at the time and had gone along with it completely. Of course, Peter came off best in the scene, as he knew he would. I was fine with it, because I knew it would help the picture.

The moment where Spartacus first meets Varinia in his cell came up on the screen. Dalton's fulsome praise of that scene made me reconsider my skepticism about how it would play. It was difficult for me, because I had to look at Jean and say the line, "I've never had a woman." Given my public image, I thought this tender moment might get a bad laugh.

Stanley left it in. He was right. (The first time test audiences were shown this scene, I held my breath. When I said the line, they accepted it completely. They didn't see Kirk Douglas playing a role—they saw Spartacus. I was dumb. I misjudged both the audience and myself.)

The next three hours went by far more quickly than they had the week before. As we approached the ending, where Peter Ustinov's character of Batiatus helps Varinia escape to freedom along with Spartacus' newborn son, I was relieved. Stanley and his editorial team—Irving Lerner and Bob Lawrence—had made some smart fixes.

One glaring problem remained. Again, Stanley was right—we needed more money to shoot additional battle sequences. For Dalton's vision of the Large Spartacus to work—a vision Stanley, Eddie, and I all shared—the audience had to actually *witness* his military prowess; it couldn't just be implied. They had to see Spartacus defeat legion after legion of Rome's finest soldiers, and the final battle scene had to be powerful enough to convey how close he had come to toppling the Roman Empire itself.

The last reel unspooled. Varinia impulsively kisses Gracchus (Charles Laughton) in gratitude for guaranteeing her safe passage out of Rome.

As Charles feared, his reply *was* cut out. His original line, written by Trumbo, was remarkably tender: "My dear young woman, I'm somewhat startled. You see, I've never had love. And I'm naturally chagrined to discover so late in my life that the having of love . . . is to set it free." The scene was still beautiful, despite the omission.

I watched, rapt, as Varinia spots her beloved Spartacus among the endless rows of crucified slaves along Appian Way. Ignoring Batiatus' warning that she shouldn't even look at him, Varinia, carrying the baby, rushes up to Spartacus on the cross. She looks up at him, tears in her eyes. The camera goes tight on her face and she holds the baby boy up for Spartacus to see.

Cut to: Varinia and the baby get in Batiatus' wagon and ride off into the sunset. We never see Spartacus on the cross! WHAT?!!

What is really *happening in this scene?*

CHAPTER TEN

"Do my choices displease you?"

—Nina Foch as Helena Glabrus

"YOU BASTARD!" THE PERSON NEAREST to me was Bob Lawrence, the assistant editor. I grabbed him in a choke hold and began screaming at him.

"Do you know how much time I spent strung up on that fucking cross? And you cut it out completely?!! You're fired!"

Eddie Lewis tried to pull me away. I shook him off. Lawrence broke free of my hold, ripping his shirt in the process. I picked up one of the folding chairs and hurled it at the rapidly retreating Stanley Kubrick.

"Goddamn it, Kubrick, you *better* run!"

Back up to the surface. These trips down into the dark waters of memory are getting harder and harder for me. I'm ashamed to remember a lot of my behavior then. Looking back, I am astounded at how much anger there was in me when I was making Spartacus. *I never wanted to be like my father, yet my rage was so much like his. I started seeing a psychiatrist to deal with my demons. They frightened even me.*

Perhaps it's possible to outlive your own anger. I think I have. My son Michael says, "Dad, you were always a softy. You just show it more now." Maybe he's right. That was the part of me that I never wanted anyone to see. I played tough guys—on- and off-camera.

The next day I sent Bob Lawrence a note of apology along with three new shirts, monogrammed with his initials.

I learned later that Stanley personally decided to remove me from the crucifixion scene, without warning me in advance. Bob Lawrence told him he was crazy—"Are you trying to get us killed?!"

That was Stanley.

The close-up of my crucifixion was cut back into the film, although like a number of other scenes, it caused us significant battles with both the studio and the censors at the Production Code Administration of the Motion Picture Association.

The correspondence back and forth with them seems laughable now. At that juncture, it was time-consuming, infuriating, and creatively destructive. Some lowlights:

> Page 1: The costumes of the slaves will have to offer adequate covering.
>
> Page 2: The whipping is in danger of proving excessively brutal.
>
> Page 8: We ask that you eliminate this particular use of the word "damn."
>
> Page 23: We ask that you eliminate the use of the word "damn."
>
> Page 24: The loincloth costumes must prove adequate.
>
> Page 27: The following line seems unduly bold and we ask that it be changed: "It's a waste of money training eunuchs."

Page 31: We recommend that you reconsider the line, "I've never had a woman . . ."

Page 45: The details of Draba's death seem excessively gruesome.

Page 72: Scenes of the men and women swimming in the nude will be unacceptable.

Page 78: The following dialogue suggests that Crassus is a sex pervert, and cannot be approved.

Page 85: The dialogue on this page clearly suggests that Crassus is sexually attracted to women and men. This flavor should be completely removed. Any suggestion that Crassus finds sexual attraction in Antoninus will have to be avoided.

Page 86: The subject of sex perversion seems to be touched on in this scene. Specifically, we note Crassus putting his hand on the boy and the boy's reaction to the gesture.

Pages 93 and 94: Any implication that Crassus is a sex pervert is unacceptable.

Page 142: The following dialogue is unacceptable: "And when this child comes out of your sweet sweet belly, I want him to be free too!"

Page 168: We cannot approve the reference to the milk stains on Varinia's gown. This includes the related dialogue by Crassus and Varinia.

Pages 200 and 201: This scene seems to suggest the danger of over-exposing Varinia while nursing her child.

Page 207: The following line suggests that Crassus is a homosexual: "Or rather, least of all, a woman."

Page 210: It would be well to avoid the nursing action, in any event, it will require most careful handling.

Page 215: We suggest you drop the use of the word "damned."

Of all these, the references to "sex perversion" were by far the most contentious. The so-called "snails and oysters scene" was where Crassus asks his body slave, Antoninus, if he has a taste for each of these culinary delicacies. The implication was that if he liked them both, he might like men as well as women.

Both Larry and Tony were intrigued and eager to play this scene, as it was a breakthrough for its time. Tony said, "The one scene with Olivier was a scene which was undoubtedly a homosexual implication . . . I liked that because that had never been done on the screen. . . ."

Here's how crazy it got. Eddie Lewis sent me a memo describing his battles with the morality police:

Dear Kirk:

I have taken one more crack at the censors on the "oysters and snails" scene. Unfortunately, their objection to this scene is based upon the one remaining strong hold of their department which is an absolute taboo against portrayal of homosexuality.

I believe they are honestly unsure that this is or is not a scene of homosexuality, but I have been unable to overcome their nervousness in this behalf. It is possible (although they will not say for certain) that they would pass the scene if we substituted "artichokes" and "truffles" for "oysters" and "snails" . . .

Artichokes and truffles?! These ridiculous disagreements were not only about moral standards regarding nudity, sex, and violence. They were also about politics—and they would come back to haunt me later, when we finally finished the film.

In the end, despite his initial objections, Stanley wound up shooting the "I am Spartacus" scene. We had only one problem. To create the impression that thousands of men were shouting "*I am Spartacus!*" we actually *needed* thousands of voices. Someone came up with the inspired idea of recording them during a nationally televised football game. Publicity and production in one play.

Young John Gavin, who played Caesar, was dispatched to Michigan State, where the Spartans (who else?) were playing the Fighting Irish of Notre Dame in front of 73,450 screaming fans.

Somehow, between hot dogs and beers, he persuaded them to chant the now-iconic line—"I am Spartacus!"—into our studio-quality tape recorders. Today, it would have just been dubbed in with the stroke of a computer key.

PS: The underdog Spartans won the game, 19–0. It was a good omen.

Eddie Muhl must have had money down on the game. Just after our crew came back from Michigan, Universal approved my request to double our budget for battle sequences, for which we had secured the use of the Spanish army. They gave us an extra half million (at $11 million, our picture alone was now worth almost exactly what Lew Wasserman paid for the entire studio lot), and we added eighteen more shooting days. Stanley and his team would spend almost the entire month of November in Spain.

Although I didn't travel to Spain, the regular reports I received were alternately alarming and encouraging. Right out of the gate, the whole thing almost fell apart. Fascist Generalissimo Francisco Franco directed his minister of the army to pull the plug, after our crew arrived in Madrid. Following a series of frantic negotiations (which I later heard involved a cash payment made directly to Franco's wife's "charity"), the shoot was back on. We hired 8,500 Spanish soldiers, paying them $8 a day, to portray both Roman warriors and rebel slaves.

The only absolute order Franco issued was that none of his soldiers be allowed to die on film. Not that he was concerned with their safety—he just didn't want us to make it *appear* as if they died. Spanish pride.

We agreed to Franco's self-glorifying condition, and Kubrick shot some extraordinary footage.

One of the most powerful scenes shot in Spain was the memorable moment when Spartacus orders his men to unleash a series of flaming brushwood cylinders down a sloping hill, directly into an advancing Roman legion. It was a vivid, amazing sequence, executed brilliantly.

To capture the scope of the battle, Stanley positioned his camera on giant, specially built towers. Many of the sequences were shot from as much as half a mile away from the actors. No one before had ever placed the camera at such a great distance from the action.

All of us—Universal included—were dazzled. Everybody agreed that the extra money was well spent. I also believe this was the moment where Stanley Kubrick came into his own as a great director. From that point on, people stopped calling him "Stanley Hubris" behind his back.

We were getting close to the end. Most of the film had been edited together, although there were still some reshoots remaining with Larry, Charles, Peter, Jean, and Tony. We would do them after the New Year.

I couldn't put off any longer the issue of who would receive screen credit for writing *Spartacus*.

In December, I called an early evening meeting with Stanley and Eddie. I knew what I intended to do and I had no doubt that Eddie would support me 100 percent. Although Dalton had pledged to tell no one about our conversation back in June, I thought it was possible that he had confided my decision to Eddie. I didn't know for certain—Eddie and I never talked about it. I didn't want to put him on the spot if someone asked him directly what my intentions were.

I opened the meeting—"So whose name are we going to put on this picture?"

Eddie responded immediately, as I knew he would, "Not mine!"

"Well, that leaves us with a problem," I said. "If your name isn't on it, we have to use Sam Jackson's name alone, and he doesn't exist. That's what happened last year with 'Robert Rich' and nobody was fooled."

"So what are you going to do?" asked Eddie.

Stanley, who so far had remained quiet, spoke up, "Why don't you use my name?"

Eddie and I looked at each other incredulously.

Stanley went on, not noticing our exchange of glances. "Why take the risk? If we put my name on it, no one will question it. I directed it, I wrote it, end of story."

I looked at Stanley. "Wouldn't you feel embarrassed putting your name on a script that someone else wrote?"

"No," said Stanley, simply. "I'm just trying to help you out."

Out of the corner of my eye I could see that Eddie was furious. I knew how deeply he felt about the injustice of the blacklist and how he hated having to play the role of the fake writer. Eddie was a man of conviction. Stanley was a man of calculation.

I adjourned the meeting. "It's late. Why don't we all just sleep on it and pick this up again in the morning?"

I went home and called Trumbo.

"Dalton, what are you doing for lunch tomorrow?"

He hesitated. It was a question I'd never asked him before. "Uh . . . I don't know. What do you have in mind?"

"If you're free, why don't you meet me at twelve thirty tomorrow at the Universal commissary?"

Silence at the other end. Dalton immediately understood the significance of my invitation.

"Be on time," I added, "and don't wear a hat."

The next day Eddie Lewis, Stanley Kubrick, and I entered the studio commissary. Walking right beside us was Dalton Trumbo. Heads were turning. People were whispering, "Is *that* Dalton Trumbo?" I even noticed a few people pointing as we were shown to our table.

The waiter came over to us immediately. "Good afternoon, Mr. Douglas. What will you gentlemen be having today?"

I said, "Let's start with my friend. What would you like, Mr. Trumbo?"

Holding the menu unsteadily in his hand, Dalton said, "You'll have to give me a minute." Then, looking down, he softly murmured, "I haven't been here in a long time."

Jean Simmons keeps the cast and crew engaged as we begin the second year of shooting Spartacus.

CHAPTER ELEVEN

"Forbid me ever to leave you."

—Jean Simmons as Varinia

JEAN SIMMONS UNWRAPPED THE MAGNUM of champagne in her dressing room. She opened the small note attached to it:

Dear Jean, I hope our second year will be as happy as our first.

Love, Kirk

It was February 19, 1960. Exactly a year before, Jean had flown in for the first time from her ranch in Arizona for her costume fitting as Varinia, leaving behind her husband, Stewart Granger, and their young daughter. A year into the picture, Jean and the rest of the cast were getting very weary. In her slave costume, she had taken to playing baseball or football with the crew, just to relieve the interminable waiting.

Laurence Olivier, Charles Laughton, and Peter Ustinov had also been required to return to Hollywood for some additional footage, or "pickups," which we needed to complete the film. Larry was once more fitted with what he self-deprecatingly described as his "Heroic Nose #137," in order to match exactly the prosthetic Roman profile he'd displayed in the scenes we shot almost twelve months earlier.

As I'd expected, there was some fallout from my decision to use Dalton's name on the picture, but the first criticism I received came from a surprising and volatile source.

Within hours of my now-widely-talked-about lunch with Trumbo in the Universal commissary, the phone rang insistently in my office.

The first call I took was from the director Otto Preminger. He was in New York preparing to make *Exodus* for United Artists. Preminger's screenwriter was Albert Maltz, another of the Unfriendly Ten who, like Trumbo, hadn't worked under his own name in more than a dozen years.

"Keerk?!" He was shouting to be understood through both the long-distance connection and his heavy German accent.

"Hello, Otto. How are you?"

"Terrible. Because of *you!*"

"Why is that, Otto?" I was calm. I knew Preminger well enough to know that he was, by his nature, a screamer. The more you yelled back, the louder he got. I was already holding the phone away from my ear and he was three thousand miles away.

"Vat are you doing?! You *know* who my writer is? It's Maltz! If you put Trumbo's name on *Spartacus*, this will kill both pictures. You cannot do this thing!"

"Otto, it's already done."

And he slammed the phone down in my ear.

But I had told Otto the truth. What was done was done. Dalton Trumbo's name would be on *Spartacus*.

Only a few weeks later, I was stunned to learn that Trumbo was going to be writing *Exodus* as well!

Not long after calling to scream at me about giving Dalton Trumbo screen credit for *Spartacus*, Preminger fired Maltz and *hired* Dalton as the new writer on *Exodus*.

The only problem was that Trumbo was under contract to write *my* next picture too, a western with Rock Hudson called *The Last Sunset*. *Exodus* was a huge project. Even for the prolific Dalton, it would be hard for him to juggle both.

I called him up immediately. "Dalton, what the hell . . . you're supposed to be writing *The Last Sunset* now, not *Exodus* for Preminger!"

"Kirk, Kirk, Kirk . . ." He was chuckling. "Remember when you fucked Otto by telling him you were using my name on *Spartacus*? Now it's *your* turn to get fucked."

I was speechless for a moment. Then I started roaring, laughing uncontrollably. Trumbo was the only man alive who could make me laugh so hard.

I shouted into the phone, "Trumbo, you two-timing, double-dealing sonofabitch—all I can say is that *Exodus* had better be good for the Jews!"

Now we were both laughing hysterically.

Otto Preminger, a talented director, had a savvy ability to use any controversy to his own advantage. In an interview with a *New York Times* reporter on January 20, two months before *Exodus* even started filming, Preminger "broke the news" that *he* would be using Dalton Trumbo's real name on the screen.

I remember saying to Anne, "You've got to hand it to Otto. He saw that the train had already left the station with *Spartacus* breaking the blacklist. Not only did he run to catch up with it, he jumped into the front car and claimed to be the engineer!"

Like doomed dinosaurs, the few remaining supporters of the

blacklist lashed out with one *final* vicious blow. And their dying tail was aimed directly at one of my best friends in the business—Frank Sinatra.

In early 1960, Frank announced, brashly and publicly, that he had hired Maltz to write the screenplay of William Bradford Huie's novel *The Execution of Private Slovik*, a true story of the only American soldier to be executed for desertion since the Civil War.

Frank was going to produce and direct it. He had never directed a film before, so this was a personally important project to him.

But his decision to pick a fight with groups like the American Legion and the Legion of Decency, as well as with powerful columnists like Hedda Hopper and Walter Winchell, was a very dangerous one.

I had quietly left a pass for Dalton at the Universal studio gate. Otto Preminger simply confirmed Trumbo's screen credit during a print interview. Sinatra was confronting the blacklist head-on, guns blazing.

With *Spartacus* in the final stages of postproduction, Frank's public fight would likely generate criticism of our film too. We would be in theaters first, several months before *Exodus*, and well before *Private Slovik* even started shooting.

The news broke about Sinatra hiring Maltz on Sunday, March 20, 1960, six months before the release of *Spartacus*. Anne and I were staying at our house in Palm Springs. Frank was our neighbor down there, but he was in Florida performing at what he called one of his "saloon gigs."

Trumbo thought the whole Sinatra/Maltz thing was a terrible idea. He called me to say so. "Kirk, Sinatra is your friend. You have to tell him *not* to do this. The politics are extremely risky—and not just for *Spartacus* or *Exodus*."

"Dalton, the first thing you need to understand about Frank is that you can't *tell* him anything. He does whatever he wants."

Trumbo ignored me as if I hadn't spoken and continued, "You have to explain to Sinatra that not only is this bad for breaking the blacklist, it's bad for the country. He's very identified with Kennedy. Nixon will use this against him. Forget about movies—the whole election could be hanging in the balance."

By now, I was used to taking Dalton's emotional exhortations with a boulder of salt, but he was making a valid point. Frank was linked closely with JFK—he'd even recorded a special Kennedy-themed version of "High Hopes" as the official campaign song.

Frank didn't care. In fact, he doubled down. He took out a full-page ad in *Daily Variety*:

> I spoke to many screenwriters, but it was not until I talked to Albert Maltz that I found a writer who saw the screenplay in exactly the terms I wanted . . . I would also like to comment on the attacks from certain quarters on Senator John Kennedy by connecting him with my decision on employing a screenwriter. This type of partisan politics is hitting below the belt. I make movies. I do not ask the advice of Senator Kennedy on whom I should hire. Senator Kennedy does not ask me how he should vote in the Senate.

I called him on the phone. "Francis, you know I love you," I began. "But *please*, go slowly. Think very carefully about what you're doing here."

"Kirkela, I've thought about *all* of it. *Very* carefully! I hate these goddamned right-wing bastards. I've hated the American Legion since I was a kid—biggest bunch of hypocrites in the country. They act like they own the flag and the rest of us are not good enough to shine their shoes."

"Yeah," I said, "but they're organized and they can cause a lot of trouble. They've got seventeen thousand chapters and they've already got Universal spooked about all of them protesting *Spartacus*."

"Fuck 'em!" Frank shouted. "When I'm through with them, they'll know they've run into the goddamnedest buzz saw they ever saw."

"So what does Kennedy say?"

Frank paused. "I haven't heard from Jack, but the Old Man called me. The Wisconsin primary is next week and it looks like they've got Humphrey beat there. But they're worried about West Virginia next month."

Over the next few weeks, the anti-Sinatra drumbeat, particularly from the Hearst papers, grew louder and louder. The New York *Daily Mirror* blasted Frank: "What kind of thinking motivates Frank Sinatra in hiring an unrepentant enemy of this country who has never done anything to remove himself from the Communist camp?"

The *New York Journal American* editorialized: "Dump Maltz and get yourself a true American writer."

Sinatra dug in his heels and fought back. When General Motors, which was sponsoring three of his television specials, threatened to pull out, he told his people, "There will be other specials."

But the die was finally cast on Tuesday, April 5. John Kennedy *did* win the Wisconsin primary, but by a smaller margin than anticipated. The "Old Man"—JFK's father, Ambassador Joseph P. Kennedy—had seen enough. He called Sinatra and said, simply, it's either "Maltz or us."

Frank took out another ad in *Variety*. It read:

In view of the reaction of my family, my friends and the American public, I have instructed my attorneys to make a settlement with Albert Maltz. I had thought that the major consideration was whether or not the script would be in the best interests of the United States. My conversations with

Maltz indicated that he has an affirmative, pro-American approach to the story. But the American public has indicated it feels the morality of hiring Maltz is the more crucial matter, and I will accept this majority opinion.

I went over to Frank's house in Palm Springs the day after that ad ran. I'd never seen him more dejected.

"Kirkela, they went after my kids. They called my kids 'Commie lovers.' My *kids*, Kirk. I can handle myself, but when they go after your kids . . ." His voice trailed off.

"I'm sorry, Frank." I didn't know what else to say.

Suddenly, his body language changed completely. His cobalt eyes, flashing like lasers, locked on me.

"You *listen* to me. They're going to try to do this to you too. Count on it. You can't let them win. Somebody has got to kick 'em in the balls until they stay down."

I just stared at him. I knew he was right. They *were* going to go after both me and *Spartacus*. They already had Sinatra's scalp. Why would they stop now?

As soon as he finished speaking, Frank's posture changed again. He seemed to shrink back, right in front of me. I felt bad for the guy.

"It wasn't me, Kirkela. I couldn't fight 'em." He put his arm around my shoulder and led me to the bar. "Maybe *you* can do it, Spartacus."

In May, I left for Mexico to shoot *The Last Sunset* with Rock Hudson. Dalton *had* finished the script. It wasn't his best work. I was right; *Exodus* had more of his attention.

While I was out of the country, opposition to *Spartacus* was mounting.

"Will Communists regain their former foothold in the American motion picture industry?" thundered the *American Legion* magazine.

In June, only weeks before John Kennedy officially became the Democratic nominee for president, the organization sent this warning to its seventeen thousand posts around the country, encouraging patriotic war veterans to protest *Spartacus* because of Trumbo's involvement:

> Dalton Trumbo has been and still is unacceptable for employment in the Motion Picture Industry under the terms of the Waldorf Declaration. Kirk Douglas has openly employed Dalton Trumbo as a Script Writer in connection with the forthcoming film "Spartacus."

Universal was getting extremely nervous. Their final investment in *Spartacus* now exceeded $12 million, and all of it was on the line. Dalton summed it up bluntly: "If the film fails, neither I nor any other blacklisted writer will ever work again."

Bryna's contract with Universal had allowed us to make the picture, but after the first press screening—scheduled for July 26—the studio had the "final cut" before distributing it. This meant the executives could, if they chose, eviscerate the picture.

In one of the most painful episodes of my entire career as an actor or producer—before or since—I watched helplessly as Universal decided to remove much of the film's potentially controversial content. Without my approval, Universal made *forty-two cuts* to the film. As Eddie Muhl later admitted, they were "for content, not for length."

Gone was the "snails and oysters" scene.

Gone was "suggestive" language like "sweet, sweet belly" and "It's a waste of money training eunuchs." But they *did* let me say "I never had a woman"—Spartacus *wasn't* a eunuch.

Gone was Charles Laughton's actual suicide scene—only the suggestion of it now remained in the film.

Gone was Bill Raisch's severed arm. This was especially galling given that I had taken such care to protect him from injury when we shot it.

And when their butchers were through cutting, we were down to just two "damns" and a single "damnation."

But it wasn't just sex, violence, and language they were after. Even more cowardly and reprehensible was what they were *really* doing in that editing room.

Having capitulated publicly on the use of Dalton Trumbo's name (the Writers Guild even gave them formal approval, making it that much harder for them to renege), Universal was now even more concerned about the *political message* of the film.

The bulk of the cuts they ordered were designed to reduce Spartacus' historical significance. Their tortured rationale was that if this rebel slave even *appeared* to have a chance at overthrowing the Roman Empire, anti-Communist critics would say that this was all part of Trumbo's hidden message designed to foment revolution in America. I'm not kidding.

"Large Spartacus," the warrior who fought for the fundamental principle that every man should be free to determine his own destiny—the same principle, by the way, on which America was founded—was reduced to, at best, "Medium Spartacus."

Although he was still depicted as more than just a runaway slave concerned only with his own safety, any hint that he might have been leading a successful revolution was removed from the film. His many victories over the Roman legions were cut out. Much of the extra footage we'd shot in Spain to depict those early victories was eliminated.

Even the simple device of showing those battles on a map, using a narrator to describe Spartacus' military successes, was deemed unacceptable by the studio.

Only the climactic battle, where Spartacus is *defeated* by Crassus, was allowed to remain in the picture.

This was Eddie Muhl's plan all along. Let Bryna make the film and let him use his executive power to make it "safe" for Universal to release.

Which they finally did on October 6, 1960, at the DeMille Theatre in New York City. I was more nervous then than at any other time in my life, except during the births of my sons. The crowd was enormous and enthusiastic. So were the first reviews:

> "ALL HAIL SPARTACUS! IT IS IN THE SAME
> GIANT CLASS AS 'BEN-HUR' . . . AND SUPERIOR
> IN WIT, CHARACTERIZATIONS AND ROMANCE!"
> —*NEW YORK POST*

> "SPARKS SEEM TO FLY FROM THE
> SCREEN! THE STORY IS THRILLING,
> FILLED WITH ACTION!"
> —*DAILY NEWS* (NEW YORK)

> "TREMENDOUS IS THE ONLY WORD
> FOR IT! EYE-POPPING . . . RARE
> DRAMATIC INTIMACY!"
> —*DAILY MIRROR* (NEW YORK)

Two weeks later we held the Hollywood premiere at the Pantages Theater. Anne took charge, organizing the entire evening as a benefit for the Women's Guild of Cedars of Lebanon Hospital. Not only did she get the studios (who were used to free tickets) to pay for their $100 seats, she got them to kick in an extra contribution directly to the charity.

ANNE: "Hi, Lew, how are you?"
WASSERMAN: "Get to the point. What do you need?"
ANNE: "I need you to take ten tickets to the premiere and

MCA to make a separate contribution to Cedars of Lebanon Hospital."

WASSERMAN: "Done. Good-bye."

In one night, she raised more than $100,000 for the hospital's free bed program. *She* was Spartacus.

When the film ended, the tuxedoed men and bejeweled women were escorted from their seats by usherettes in slave costumes (the irony, sad to say, was lost on most of the guests) to an after party at the Beverly Hilton Hotel.

Bob Hope, not exactly a political radical, was the master of ceremonies. He had a lot of fun skewering me: "This is the best picture Kirk Douglas has made since he grew his other ear . . . I thought Kirk was much braver in this one than in *The Vikings— eight million dollars* braver!"

Throughout the night, there were no more than ten pickets, including one man named "Uncle Sam" who was in striped red, white, and blue trousers. In other words, the American Legion had bullied and blustered, but ultimately they were just bluffing.

"Honey," I said, after we took one last spin around the dance floor at 2:30 a.m., "let's go home. I'm tired. And the next time I tell you that I want to make a big costume epic, will you please just shoot me?"

She smiled sweetly. "Kirk, if you ever make another one of these, I will leave you."

"If you leave me," I said, kissing her lightly on the lips, "I'm going with you."

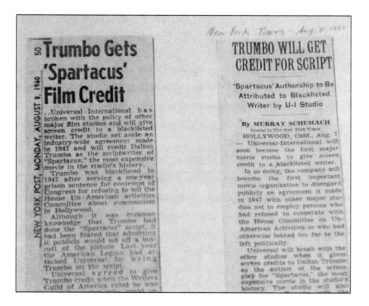

New York Times - Aug. 8 1960

Trumbo Gets 'Spartacus' Film Credit

NEW YORK POST, MONDAY, AUGUST 1, 1960

Universal - International has broken with the policy of other major film studios and will give screen credit to a blacklisted writer. The studio set aside an industry-wide agreement made in 1947 and will credit Dalton Trumbo as the scriptwriter of "Spartacus," the most expensive movie in the studio's history.

Trumbo was blacklisted in 1947 after serving a one-year prison sentence for contempt of Congress for refusing to tell the House Un-American Activities Committee about communism in Hollywood.

Although it was common knowledge that Trumbo had done the "Spartacus" script, it had been feared that admitting it publicly would set off a boycott of the picture. Last year the American Legion had attacked Universal for using Trumbo on the script.

Universal agreed to give Trumbo credit when the Writers Guild of America ruled he was

TRUMBO WILL GET CREDIT FOR SCRIPT

'Spartacus' Authorship to Be Attributed to Blacklisted Writer by U-I Studio

By MURRAY SCHUMACH
Special to The New York Times

HOLLYWOOD, Calif., Aug. 7 — Universal-International will soon become the first major movie studio to give screen credit to a blacklisted writer.

In so doing, the company will become the first important movie organization to disregard publicly an agreement it made in 1947 with other major studios not to employ persons who had refused to cooperate with the House Committee on Un-American Activities or who had otherwise leaned too far to the left politically.

Universal will break with the other studios when it gives screen credits to Dalton Trumbo as the author of the screen play for "Spartacus," the most expensive movie in the studio's history. The studio will also

The blacklist is broken.

CHAPTER TWELVE

"For years, your family and mine have been members of the Equestrian Order and the Patrician Party. Servants and rulers of Rome. Why have you left us for Gracchus and the mob?"

—Laurence Olivier as Marcus Crassus

DURING THE FIRST WEEK OF February 1961, Paul B. "Red" Fay was living alone. Newly appointed as the undersecretary of the navy, Fay was staying at the Army-Navy Club while waiting for his family to join him in Washington, D.C.

The phone rang on Wednesday morning, February 1. The receptionist buzzed him. Nervously, she said, "Mr. Fay, I have the president for you."

"Grand Old Lovable," boomed the Boston-accented voice, using the nickname he'd given Fay when they served together on a PT boat during World War II. "How would you like to see *Spartacus* on Friday night with the president of the United States?"

"Mr. President," said Fay, "I'm with you all the way."

"All right," said Kennedy. "It's playing at the Warner Theatre. Get a couple of good seats for Friday night, but don't let anyone know who they are for. If there is a crowd out there to greet us, I'm going to have your top secret clearance removed. Be over here at seven p.m. for a quick dinner."

"Here" was the White House.

The black Lincoln limousine pulled up in front of D.C.'s historic Warner Theatre shortly after 8:00 p.m. on a stormy Friday night. In giant letters, the theater's marquee read:

SPARTACUS!
Starring Kirk Douglas, Laurence Olivier, Jean Simmons, Charles Laughton, Peter Ustinov, John Gavin, and Tony Curtis

Although the trip was only four short blocks from the White House, the persistent snow combined with sleet made for treacherous driving on the icy streets.

There were still a few American Legion protesters shivering outside the theater on that cold Friday night, but the blizzard-like conditions made it impossible for them to see inside the car. When it came to a stop, four Secret Service men jumped out onto the snow-covered sidewalk, one of them holding the door open for its two remaining passengers.

First out of the car was Red Fay. Although his body was buried under layers of warm clothing, Fay's face stung painfully as he was struck by a blast of the frigid night air.

Following immediately behind him, and shoving Fay quickly toward the warm lobby of the waiting theater, was John Fitzgerald Kennedy.

Exactly two weeks earlier, in weather just as cold, he had taken the oath of office as the thirty-fifth president of the

United States, vowing "to preserve, protect, and defend the Constitution of the United States."

The president grimaced briefly when he saw the theater manager and his assistant standing on the street waiting for them. But it wasn't Fay's fault. The Secret Service must have contacted the theater on its own.

As the manager escorted them through the empty lobby, the president said, "We don't want to disturb the audience. Can't we just go right down to our seats without any commotion?"

"That's all right, Mr. President. We've stopped the film for you. It's only been on for a few minutes. We'll start it again when you and Mr. Fay are seated."

JFK winced again, but managed to say, "Thank you. I appreciate your kindness." This was exactly what he hadn't wanted.

The doors opened and the four Secret Service men filed in ahead of Kennedy and Fay, blocking the audience from seeing their faces by the light from the lobby. The theater itself was still completely dark, yet the sound of rhythmic clapping began as soon as the president started walking down the aisle.

"Amazing," whispered Red Fay. "They're even applauding for you in the dark."

"That's not for *me*, Grand Old Lovable," replied the president. "They want the film turned back on. C'mon, let's sit down."

The manager directed them to their two seats in the center of the theater, eight rows from the back. The rest of the aisle was completely empty, as were all the rows behind them. The Secret Service had seen to that.

The clapping was growing louder. There was hooting and whistling and a few catcalls. "We want our money back," one man shouted.

"You're right, Redhead, that *is* for me," the president said with a grin as they sat down.

The four agents settled in directly behind them, and as if by some hidden cue, the film immediately started running again—but it had been rewound back to the beginning. There were groans and some additional catcalls from the audience, but the theater quickly grew quiet as Alex North's magnificent score once more filled the room.

During the opening titles, the president spotted someone familiar sitting directly in front of him—Orville Freeman, the secretary of agriculture, along with his wife. Tapping him lightly on the shoulder, he leaned forward and asked, "Haven't the leaders of the New Frontier got anything better to do with their time than spend it going to the movies?"

Freeman, a former governor of Minnesota who had experience answering tough questions, responded without hesitation, "I wanted to be immediately available on a moment's notice if the president wanted me." Kennedy laughed, and then they all turned their attention to the screen.

As "Screenplay by Dalton Trumbo" flashed across the giant screen, the president elbowed his friend. "I once met some Trumbos in Ireland. Do you think he's Irish? I hope so." Even in the flickering light of the projector, Fay could see the twinkle in Kennedy's eye.

For the next three and half hours, Kennedy and Fay watched the film, engrossed in the story. From time to time, Kennedy would nudge his friend, saying things like "Look at *that* guy" and "Amazing acting."

For JFK, an avid student of history, these were all familiar characters. Even before seeing the picture, he knew the story of Spartacus' slave revolt, as well as numerous details of the lives of Roman leaders like Caesar, Crassus, and Gracchus.

As the final credits rolled, the audience was applauding once more.

This time it was for the film. Then the lights came on and the people in the front half of the theater turned around and saw the president of the United States putting on his coat and scarf.

The applause became thunderous. Kennedy nodded and

smiled, waving slightly to the crowd. "It was a fine picture, don't you think?" The crowd cheered its agreement.

The president and Red Fay walked out through the lobby. Kennedy took a brochure, "Spartacus, the Rebel Against Rome," and stuck it in the pocket of his overcoat.

Back in the car, the president turned to his friend. "Bobby was right." He smiled. "It *was* a good film. I should take his advice more often."

The limousine drove slowly off into the now-clear night. The storm had passed.

Released!

EPILOGUE

"When a free man dies, he loses the pleasure of life; a slave loses its pain. Death is the only freedom a slave knows. That's why he's not afraid of it. That's why we'll win."

—Kirk Douglas as Spartacus

Back up for air, this time to stay. It was very difficult writing about something that happened over half a century ago. You are amazed at how much you've forgotten and fascinated when you read the research and discover the thousands of details that go into the making of a motion picture. It's an interesting process.

When I sat down to write this book, I watched Spartacus *from beginning to end for the first time since 1960. I saw a young man up on the screen. I was a very different person fifty years ago. You can't imagine the changes that occur in a human being as you get older. I was surprised by how headstrong I was back then, and yet that's probably what helped me to make* Spartacus.

People point to it as the moment the Hollywood blacklist was finally broken. But as I said at the beginning of this book, I didn't set out to make a statement—I was just trying to make the best picture I could about a story that mattered to me. It still does.

What Spartacus *really shattered was the "hypocrisy list." Many blacklisted writers were working during that horrendous time; they just couldn't tell anyone. They also had to accept wages that were a fraction of what they earned under their real names. Imagine what that does to a man, particularly a creative man. Dalton Trumbo said to me, "Kirk, thank you for giving me back my name."*

It shouldn't have been mine to give—no one, certainly not the government, should have the power to deprive a man of his birthright. That was the hypocrisy of the blacklist. We all knew it was going on and most decent Americans knew it was wrong, but we pretended that it didn't matter. You did what you had to do.

If Spartacus *helped change that shameful practice—where indifference became a substitute for integrity—I am proud of that. Others, particularly Eddie Lewis and Otto Preminger, deserve great credit too— they fought for what they knew was right, even when it wasn't popular.*

Most of the cast of Spartacus *is now gone. That's hard for me to write about.*

Yet our personal and professional lives were all profoundly affected by the three years it took for Spartacus *to reach the screen.*

Old marriages ended and new ones began. Shortly after the film's release, Laurence Olivier's twenty-year marriage to Vivien Leigh mercifully came to an end. A few months later, Larry and Joan Plowright eloped to Connecticut. They had three children and remained happily married until his death in 1989.

In 1991, we discovered that the deleted "snails and oysters" scene was still in the Universal vault. The problem was that the audio track was unusable. Tony Curtis came in and redubbed his Antoninus lines, more than thirty years after they were originally recorded. With graciousness and inspiration, Joan Plowright suggested that Anthony Hopkins might be called upon to redo her late husband's lines, as

Hopkins did a superb impression of Olivier. So now, when Crassus asks Antoninus if "taste is not the same as appetite," the speaking voice you hear belongs to Sir Anthony Hopkins. He did an uncanny job. Listen carefully to Olivier in the other scenes—I'll bet you can't tell the difference.

In 1960, Jean Simmons filed for divorce from Stewart Granger. Within months she, too, remarried—this time to writer/director Richard Brooks, who directed her that same year in Elmer Gantry. *My darling Jean passed away last year, still as lovely and elegant as the day we met.*

Charles Laughton never sued me, and we became friendly again over our shared passion for art. He was brilliantly knowledgeable about painting and was always gracious in sharing his keen opinions with Anne and me. When Charles was diagnosed with cancer in 1962, I wrote to him in the hospital. It touched me to learn that he kept that letter among his personal papers, which were donated to UCLA.

Our dear friends Tony Curtis and Janet Leigh divorced in 1962. I was best man at Tony's wedding to a young German actress named Christine. The marriage didn't last, but our friendship did. I was an honorary pallbearer at his funeral in 2010. I miss him still.

John Gavin left acting permanently in 1981, when President Reagan appointed him as United States ambassador to Mexico. Anne and I went out with him and his lovely wife, Connie Towers, just a few weeks ago. At eighty, John is still as strong and handsome as he was when he played the young Caesar. There's been only one noticeable change in his appearance since Spartacus. *He noted it wryly over dinner—"Kirk, your hair turned white. Mine turned loose."*

Spartacus *was not nominated for a Best Picture Oscar—maybe the voters were more conservative than the general public—but Oscar night was still amusing, especially when Russell Metty won for Best Cinematography. After having essentially been told by Stanley to sit down and shut up for more than a year, he got to give an acceptance speech for his fine "work." I don't remember if he thanked Stanley.*

Peter Ustinov did *win an Oscar for Best Supporting Actor for his role in* Spartacus. *This was particularly funny to me, since for months he'd been regaling the Hollywood party circuit with this bon mot: "The problem in* Spartacus *is to be good without being too good." The implication, of course, was that he couldn't risk outshining the boss.*

It didn't bother me a bit, because I knew Peter couldn't resist a witty line. And it was funny. I still laugh when I remember him today. Anne adored him too.

Lew Wasserman finally bought Universal Studios in 1962. He became my landlord and my boss, but he always remained my friend. His vision for a Universal City has been realized beyond anyone's wildest dreams. People remember Lew as a mogul. I remember him as a mensch whose word was his bond.

Stanley Kubrick and I continued to have a complicated history over the next four decades. His bitterness over not having had total control over every frame of Spartacus *plagued him throughout his life. When Stanley listed all the pictures he had directed, he always omitted* Spartacus. *It was the thorn in his side. He said things like "Spartacus had everything but a good story." And "I don't know what to say when someone tells me 'Spartacus is my favorite movie.'"*

Yet only a few years after we parted ways, I received a very thoughtful letter from him—out of the blue—offering several constructive suggestions for my production of Seven Days in May. *I came across the letter recently in my files and it made me remember that despite his tremendous difficulty in empathizing with people, he was obsessed with perfection in storytelling—even someone else's story. Stanley was an extraordinary talent, and I am grateful that our paths crossed.*

There's one more strange connection between Kubrick and me that I've never told anyone about before. When we were having problems on Spartacus, *I once took him with me to one of my regular appointments with Dr. Herbert Kupper, my psychiatrist. In those days, it wasn't uncommon to use your therapy visits to help work out specific problems—and Stanley and I had more than a few issues that could use a professional referee.*

I can't tell you that it helped our working relationship—but Dr. Kupper did make one suggestion to Stanley that had a tangible result in his life. He recommended a book—a 1926 German novella, Traumnovelle *by Arthur Schnitzler—that he thought would make a good movie. Forty years later, that book was the basis for Stanley's final film,* Eyes Wide Shut.

Of all the people I worked with on Spartacus, *Dalton Trumbo was unique. He was more of a character than most of the actors I've known. He was a man who loved life. He loved living it, he loved describing it, he loved affecting it. Opinionated to a fault, yet never offended when challenged, he was that rare combination of self-confidence leavened with self-deprecation. To take your work seriously without taking yourself seriously is a rare gift—and Dalton had it in spades.*

Two years later we worked together on Lonely Are the Brave *—the best script I've ever read. It required no revisions. We shot it exactly as he wrote it, and I still believe the character of Jack Burns is the best role I've ever played.*

My friend "Sam" taught me a lot about courage and grace. I hope this book will help Dalton Trumbo be remembered as the true American hero he was.

Our world, I am sad to say, still remains divided today over many of the same issues that we lived through during the Red Scare and the making of Spartacus. *Fearmongers Gerald L. K. Smith and Hedda Hopper have been replaced by a new generation of demagogues like Rush Limbaugh. The fight for basic human freedom depicted in* Spartacus *is going on all over the globe from Syria to Iran.*

I believe much of the divisiveness in the world has been caused by religion, even in the time of Spartacus when they worshipped many gods. What is the purpose of religion? After ninety-five years on this planet, I have come to the conclusion that religion should be based on only one thing: helping your fellow man. If everybody followed that religion—helping his fellow man—armies would vanish overnight. Injustice, intolerance, and inhumanity would disappear. And blacklists would never be written. What a wonderful world that would be.

And what a wonderful world it sometimes is. I am thinking back to March 20, 1991—a very special night. The room was filled; the Screen Writers Guild was honoring me for breaking the blacklist. I went back to my table with the award and showed it to my beloved Anne.

Everybody gave me congratulations and we went home. As we were lying in bed, I nudged my wife—"Honey, wasn't that a wonderful evening? Weren't you proud to hear him say all those nice things about me breaking the blacklist?"

She didn't answer.

I sat up in bed. "Honey, I really think I did something historic."

Anne looked at me—"Yes, but what have you done lately?" Then she turned out the light. Even in the dark, I knew there was a big smile on her face.

IMAGE GALLERY

IN FRONT OF THE CAMERA

Kirk Douglas as Spartacus

Batiatus (Peter Ustinov) inspects Spartacus.

Marcellus
(Charles McGraw)
brands Spartacus.

Spartacus and
Varinia
(Jean Simmons)

Marcellus (Charles McGraw) identifies the target points on Spartacus.

Spartacus chokes Marcellus (Charles McGraw).

Spartacus leads the escape.

Spartacus leaps to freedom.

Foreground: Marcus Crassus (Laurence Olivier); background: Batiatus (Peter Ustinov)

Sempronius Gracchus (Charles Laughton) and Julius Caesar (John Gavin)

*Spartacus leads a surprise attack
on the Roman camp.*

Spartacus with his troops

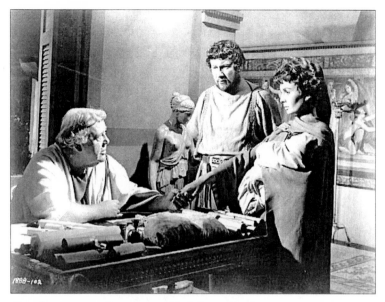

Gracchus grants safe passage to Varinia and Batiatus.

Spartacus and Varinia ("I've never had a woman.")

Varinia in the water (Jean said to me: "I bet you've had a lot of experience getting girls to take off their bras.")

Varinia and Spartacus

Spartacus

Crassus

Slaves into battle!

Hand-to-hand combat

"I am Spartacus!"

*Antoninus (Tony Curtis) and Spartacus
("Are you afraid to die, Spartacus?")*

*Spartacus crucified
("This is your son. He's free, Spartacus! Free!")*

Final thoughts

BEHIND THE SCENES

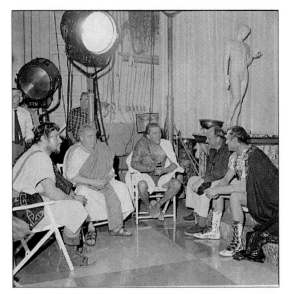

The cast assembles. Left to right: Peter Ustinov (Batiatus); Charles Laughton (Gracchus); me (Spartacus); director Anthony Mann; Laurence Olivier (Crassus)

Sabina Bethman's brief moment of stardom

Wearing my producer's robe

Laurence Olivier visits the desert set on our first day of shooting.

Peter Ustinov,
the Clown Prince

Making a point to
Eddie Lewis and
Laurence Olivier

Giving Janet Leigh a tour of the Spartacus *set*

Good times with Jean and Tony

Stanley Kubrick, a young man with a mission

The many faces of Charles Laughton

Trapped in a film of my own making

Between takes with my friend Jean

Peter, Charles, and Jean

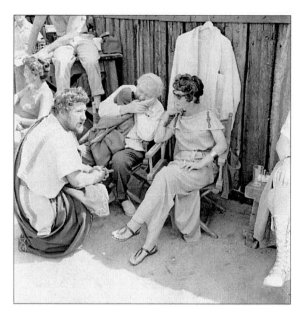

A long day for Laurence

Laurence Olivier with Tracy Granger (and her mother, Jean Simmons)

A funny thing happened on the way to the Forum . . . damned if I know what it was! Left to right: John Gavin, Peter Ustinov, Tony Curtis, Laurence Olivier, and me

Jean Simmons relaxes with her husband, Stewart Granger.

Spartacus enters the arena.

Spartacus and Draba (Woody Strode) fight to the death.

Watching the warriors

Jean Simmons and Stanley Kubrick

Hedda Hopper graces us with a set visit. (Later she would declare that "Spartacus *was written by a Commie and the screen script was written by a Commie, so don't go see it.*")

Spartacus — *Cast Portrait*
*Left to right: me, Laurence Olivier, Jean Simmons, Peter Ustinov, John Gavin,
Nina Foch, John Dall, Joanna Barnes, John Ireland,
Charles McGraw, and Tony Curtis*

ACKNOWLEDGMENTS

BELLS WERE RINGING, HORNS WERE tooting, people were shouting, all to usher in the New Year, 2012, in Times Square.

Three thousand miles away, David Bender, my research editor, turned down the volume on the TV in my living room in Montecito, California. He had a paper in his hand. What was he reading on New Year's Eve? It was a foreword to this book written by George Clooney that had just arrived that morning. I hadn't seen it yet.

When David finished reading it, I was flabbergasted. I don't know George Clooney—I have only spoken with him once on the telephone. I've been a fan of his since he played a doctor on *ER*.

Yet what I admire most about George Clooney is how he uses his tremendous visibility to support humanitarian efforts all over the world.

I thank him deeply for his kind and gracious words.

The president of Universal, Ron Meyer, and his staff, particularly archivist Jeff Pirtle, opened their vaults, files, and hearts to this project. Many of the photos you see in this book had never before been developed and appear here for the first time. That they even found them at all is a miracle to me, but then, Ron is a miracle man.

My publicist, Marcia Newberger, told me this was an important story, worth telling. I'm glad she is as persuasive as she is talented.

To all the people at Open Road Integrated Media—the dynamic Jane Friedman, the supportive Richard Florest, the extraordinarily able Nicole Passage, and my thoughtful and insightful editor, George Hodgman—thank you for taking a two-thousand-year-old story that was brought to life on-screen more than half a century ago and turning it into a twenty-first-century book. And my thanks to Jim Kohlberg for first introducing this project to Open Road.

I want to express my appreciation to Dame Joan Plowright for suggesting Sir Anthony Hopkins record the lines originally spoken by her late husband, Lord Laurence Olivier, in order to restore the famously censored "snails and oysters" scene. The film is now much closer to the one we shot—and for that I am deeply grateful.

The film *Spartacus* reflects the efforts of so many people. It's impossible to thank all of them, but I especially want to thank my producer, Eddie Lewis, who first brought me the book. There were many days when neither of us thought the movie would ever get made.

I am very grateful for the cooperation of Maxine Ducey and the staff at the Center for Film and Theater Research at the University of Wisconsin, where my papers are housed.

I am glad that my wife, Anne, and our long-time friend and assistant, Fifi, compiled everything during the three years it took to make *Spartacus*—resulting in a huge scrapbook containing hundreds of clippings from all over the world.

When you write a story about something that happened fifty or sixty years ago, you learn (and relearn) a lot about yourself. My research editor, David Bender, delved into all my files at the University of Wisconsin and Universal Studios, as well as my scrapbooks. I was delighted to discover how much fun it was working with him while I traveled back in time to write this book. His assistance was indispensable to me.

I want to thank my assistant, Grace Eboigbe, the only person capable of transmitting my spoken or written words. Thanks also to Jeff Conway, John Gavin, Lee Grant, Angel McConnell, and Sam Vinal for kindly helping to make this book happen.

I am grateful to my children—Michael and his wife, Catherine; Joel and his wife, JoAnn; and Peter and his wife, Lisa—for their love and support. I remember Eric every day.

To my grandchildren, Cameron, Kelsey, Tyler, Ryan, Jason, Carys, and Dylan—Pappy loves you all very much.

About the Author

KIRK DOUGLAS IS A RENOWNED actor who appeared in over ninety movies before retiring from film acting in 2004. His work on and off the screen has been rewarded with three Academy Award nominations, an Oscar for Lifetime Achievement, and the Medal of Freedom. Through his production company, Bryna, he has produced acclaimed films such as *The Vikings, Lonely Are the Brave, Paths of Glory,* and *Seven Days in May.* A master storyteller, Douglas has also penned ten novels and memoirs. In 2009, he starred in an autobiographical one-man show called *Before I Forget* at the Center Theatre Group's Kirk Douglas Theatre in Los Angeles. Douglas maintains an active life in Beverly Hills and Montecito, where he resides with his beloved wife, Anne.

copyright © 2012 by the Bryna Company

cover design by Andrea C. Uva

Unless otherwise noted, all images courtesy of Universal Studios Licensing LLC, photos taken by Dick Miller and William Reed (Globe Photos)

ISBN: 978-1-4532-5480-6

Published in 2012 by Open Road Integrated Media
180 Varick Street
New York, NY 10014
www.openroadmedia.com

()

CPSIA information can be obtained at www.ICGtesting.com
Printed in the USA
BVOW070737220512

290739BV00001B/9/P

9 781453 254806